The Innovative School Librarian

Thinking outside the box

The Innovative School Librarian

Thinking outside the box

Sharon Markless, editor
Elizabeth Bentley, Sarah Pavey,
Sue Shaper, Sally Todd, Carol Webb

facet publishing

Published by Facet Publishing,
7 Ridgmount Street, London WC1E 7AE
www.facetpublishing.co.uk

Facet Publishing is wholly owned by CILIP:
the Chartered Institute of Library and
Information Professionals.

British Library Cataloguing in Publication Data
A catalogue record for this book is available
from the British Library.

ISBN 978-1-85604-653-4

First published 2009

Text printed on PEFC
accredited material. The policy
of Facet Publishing is to use

PEFC
PEFC/16-33-111
CATG-PEFC-052
www.pefc.org

papers that are natural,
renewable and recyclable
products, made from wood
grown in sustainable forests. In the
manufacturing process of our books, and to
further our policy, preference is given to
printers that have FSC and PEFC Chain of
Custody certification. The FSC and/or
PEFC logos will appear on those books
where full certification has been granted to
the printer concerned.

Typeset from editors' disks by Facet
Publishing in 12/17 pt Aldine 401 and URW
Grotesk.
Printed and made in Great Britain by MPG
Books Ltd, Bodmin, Cornwall.

Contents

Foreword ix

How to read this book xi

Acknowledgements xii

Part 1 Who is the librarian? 1

1   Professionalism and the school librarian. 1

What are the discourses of professionalism?. 4

Discourse of managerialism 4

Discourse of technical-rationalism 9

Discourse of social democracy 11

Where does this leave school librarianship in the 21st century?. . . . 15

What influences the school librarian's professional identity? 18

Our professional identity 22

2   How others see us. 25

Who are the significant others?. 27

Within the school community 27

Outside the school 34

What influences the perceptions of these significant stakeholders?. . 36

How do school librarians think the stakeholders see them?. 41

What are the implications of the perceptions of the librarian?. 44

Conclusion 45

3   **Bridging the gap** 47
     Is there always a dichotomy?. 47
     In what circumstances might a dichotomy arise? 49
     How can we resolve the dichotomy?. 55

Part 2 **Your community: from perceptions to practice**. **61**
4   **Identifying and understanding your community**. **61**
     How do we define our community?. 62
     What informs the ways we explore our community?. 64
     Ways of thinking about your learning community 66
     What does learning look like in our own institutions?. 69
     What does learning look like for the individuals in our own
     communities?. 73

5   **Making a positive response**. **77**
     Getting into position. 77
     What is possible in the real world of school libraries? 78
     Staying positive 80
     Using evidence to support your case 83
     Benchmarking between school libraries. 83
     Learning from the world. 86
     Making a difference 88
     Tapping in to school and user priorities. 89
     How do we make line-management systems work for us?. 92
     How do we use other relationships to help us?. 95
     Learning from the students 97
     What if our personal vision does not match the library reality? 99
     How do we know if we are meeting the needs of our community?. . 100
     How well are we doing? 101

Part 3 **Moving forward**. **103**
6   **Inspiration** **103**
     What is inspiration? 103
     Where does inspiration fit into school librarianship? 103

At what levels can inspiration operate? 107

How do we keep ourselves inspired? 111

Inspiration from inside ourselves. 113

Inspiration from inside the school. 114

Inspiration from outside the school. 115

What has inspired us?. 119

Reality check 121

Inspiring others 122

7   Becoming integral to teaching and learning. 127

But what does integration mean? 127

Becoming an integral part of the teaching team 128

Beyond information skills 131

Possible starting points 132

Sustaining integration into teaching and learning 134

Becoming integral to the structure of the school 135

Pathways to integration at school level 139

8   Innovation 143

Connect 144

Act 146

Evidence. 149

Managing change. 151

Process and principles of managing change. 153

Using whole-school processes and the key change agents 154

References. 157

Websites cited 166

Appendix 1 Levels of education. 167

Appendix 2 School library self-evaluation questions 168

Appendix 3 Sample survey of teachers' perceptions of the role of the
school librarian. 170

Appendix 4 SWOT analysis 171

Appendix 5 Choosing priorities in development planning –
sample grid 173

Appendix 6 An example of a completed self-evaluation. 174

Appendix 7 Some possibilities for gaining inspiration in the UK . . . 176

Appendix 8 Tools for managing change 180

Appendix 9 Managing change: process and principles. 181

Index. 187

Foreword

Katya received a visit by fellow librarians to see the new school library. She prepared for the visit by displaying information on all her most recent activities to demonstrate how the library contributed to assessment for learning, reader development, teaching of 16–18 year olds and staff training. Katya observed that her visitors wanted to look at her stock and her general displays and to discuss how she managed overdue books. Several times she drew their attention to the information that showcased her wider activities but the majority of her visitors remained focused on the room's resources and its management rather than moving to a discussion of teaching and learning.

This book was written to prompt school librarians to stand back from their day-to-day activity and critically re-examine their values, philosophy and what defines their professional practice. It focuses on ways of thinking about the job of school librarian rather than on its operational responsibilities. There are big differences between schools: different curricula, different patterns of governance and management; and different levels and types of resources before we even get to the students and teachers. This inevitably leads to big differences between school libraries. However, through working internationally with colleagues from the USA, Australia, Sweden, Denmark, Lithuania and Portugal, we know that school librarians share many common concerns as well as a common vision of what we are trying to achieve.

We therefore believe that this book has wide relevance. It addresses principles and issues that all school librarians need to confront during their career, whatever their context. So, although all the authors are school librarians working in the UK, we believe that the ideas in the book are not confined to the UK.

We invite you to take what you want from this book and adapt the ideas to your own context. We are not trying to provide solutions to your everyday problems. We are challenging you as a school librarian to think more widely, to be strategic and to move outside your comfort zone into the heart of teaching and learning in your school. But we are also challenging you to do this in a way that connects deeply to your underpinning beliefs about the role of the school library. To this end, the book raises issues to consider, questions to pose, and approaches to analysing your role as school librarian. We hope that this will enable you to examine your practice critically and find the innovative responses that will work for you.

We have tried to illuminate the ideas in this book through vignettes that present some real experiences of school librarians. We hope that the vignettes will resonate with you and enable you to look afresh at elements of your own practice. The vignettes may indicate a way forward. However, they are not meant to be blueprints for action nor do we use them to suggest that everyone will find themselves in the situations outlined.

This book was collaboratively written by five school librarians and a lecturer in higher education. The school librarians work in very different environments (schools with different types of students, different rationales for the school library, different roles for the school library, different priorities and different governance). This collaboration involved us in a sustained quest for clarity and understanding. The process of collaboration forced us to share our assumptions, examine our prejudices and justify our interpretations. Effective collaboration is not about gaining consensus, but about crafting something more than can be achieved individually. Our different realities have been brought to bear on each chapter. The challenge has been to find significant things to say that all of us are happy to subscribe to.

How to read this book

We hope that you will read the chapters in this book in the order that they are presented. This is because we believe that coming to think and act differently is a cumulative experience; we have therefore constructed this book as a narrative designed to lead the reader through a succession of issues, culminating in the chapter on innovation, which we see as the key to renewing and refreshing our professional identities.

Sharon Markless (editor), Elizabeth Bentley, Sarah Pavey,
Sue Shaper, Sally Todd, Carol Webb

Acknowledgements

We would like to thank Anne Felton for her invaluable contributions at the beginning of this long process. We are very sorry that she was unable to continue with us to the completion of this book.

Several of the vignettes arose from discussions on the School Librarians' Network (SLN) an online discussion forum. Many thanks to everyone who contributed.

We would like to thank David Streatfield for his helpful contributions when reading the draft version of this book.

1 Professionalism and the school librarian

Why is professionalism important to us? It is a topic hotly debated throughout all library sectors and across many fields such as health, law and commerce, because it is linked to ideas of status, conduct and quality of service. This chapter will examine professionalism, because we believe it goes to the heart of our work identities.

Not all schools round the world, or closer to the home of the authors in the UK, are fortunate enough to have a library. As in many countries, school libraries in the UK are not a statutory requirement, resulting in a mix of provision. Equally not all school libraries are run by professional librarians. They may be run by teachers, teaching assistants, clerical assistants, or library managers. Even where there is a professionally managed library the person running it may be a dually qualified teacher/librarian (a common pattern in the USA and Australia) or a singly professionally qualified librarian. A significant minority of secondary schools and a few primary schools in the UK employ such professionals, who are referred to as chartered librarians when they have successfully completed their course of study and the qualification process afterwards. There is no single set of qualifications or experience for the job and traditional distinctions between professional and non-professional staff are not acceptable in today's workforce. Where such fragmentation exists, homogeneity of standards is not a realistic goal at present, although the professional organization for librarians in the UK – the Chartered Institute for Library and Information Professionals (CILIP) – is moving towards a framework of qualifications and accreditation which covers the whole spectrum of those working in our field. We are now all at different stages on the same road of continuing professional development.

Where then does that leave notions of professionalism? This diversity means that we cannot think about professionalism in terms of qualifications, experience or the promise of statutory status. To do so would exclude many who currently run school libraries. So we must find other ways to think about professionalism.

The value and meaning attached to the concept of professionalism ebbs and flows. Today footballers are referred to as 'professional', indicating that they are paid for what they do, as opposed to amateurs who play for pleasure. On the other hand a professional was traditionally distinguished from a craftsperson, by mastery of the intellectual aspects of their role. Today's workforce is much more complex, with a web of career pathways and a recognition that professional development is a continuing journey, where passing one exam or hurdle does not mean that you have 'arrived'. Technological advances, organizational change and the advent of the digital generation are blurring the picture and challenging accepted ideas of professionalism.

The struggle for professional recognition is not new; it is why people form associations. Nonetheless, just as individuals have faced threats to their identity so have these associations. People no longer remain within one career for their entire working lives and so fields of employment contract and expand and this is reflected in changing membership numbers. Centralizing resources and stabilizing membership figures has become a matter of survival. Consequently the 21st century has seen a number of amalgamations. For example, in 2002 the Library Association and the Institute of Information Scientists in the UK merged to form CILIP.

It has been claimed that a profession never talks so much about being professional, nor strives so hard for recognition as a profession, as when it feels itself to be under threat (Stronach et al., 2002). One way forward is to think about the different discourses of professionalism. These give us clues about what professional practice looks like and what we are doing when we act professionally. There are lots of different models and each has strengths and weaknesses. They help us to see ourselves as professionals in our schools and give us ways of moving forward. Their influences help determine our priorities for how time and money should be spent in service provision. The discourses that follow are not just about school librarianship but are relevant to all library sectors in all parts of the world. This matter has been considered by Carol Kuhlthau (1993), a well known American researcher and champion of school libraries. As you can see in Appendix 1, her research identified a series of roles for school librarians and, although a little dated, these still resonate with us today.

What are the discourses of professionalism?

Discourse in this sense refers to the power of language and how it shapes our practice and identity. This happens daily within our institutions where language is a reflection of the organization's accepted thinking. It is used to drive its policies and so shape our behaviour and responses. On a larger scale it is a mechanism used in the formation of policy by governments to solicit support and compliance. The study of discourse is mainly derived from the work of the French philosopher Michel Foucault (1972). The significance of discourse is easily recognized in education where the use of language continually evolves to influence people's attitudes and behaviour. For instance, a 'disaffection project' becomes a 'behaviour improvement programme' or 'remedial studies' becomes 'learning support' or 'inclusion' (and, in the school library world, the 'school library' becomes a 'learning centre' or evolves across the Atlantic as a 'media resource center'). The following discourses are considered and their effects on professionalism in school libraries explored in turn.

Discourse of managerialism

This is typically an externally imposed model; it is not about individuals negotiating what they want to do. They may have some say in types of target-setting but generally this is done to other people's expectations. This discourse emphasizes the manager's role as instilling accountability into the organization's culture. The discourse of managerialism is usually identified with the methods of the private sector that have been transferred to the public sector to encourage a culture of efficiency and economy. It aims to encourage conduct and activities that are considered appropriate in a market environment, believing the market mechanism to be the best driver of effectiveness. This is done by linking evaluation processes and performance review to value for money.

In education, this is in the arena of national curricula and publication of exam result league tables coupled with a system of inspection to monitor implementation. Knowledge of how we will be evaluated influences our behaviour, hence the pressure that teachers feel to 'teach to the test' rather than give attention to topics or skills that they might consider more appropriate for their students. School development plans, now repackaged as school improvement plans, could be seen as an outcome of the managerialist discourse, in that they allocate resources to desired changes which are linked to central government priorities. This level of prescription and setting of common standards is criticized for reducing the level of autonomy available to teachers and librarians. Others see this as a method of achieving change for the better, in a manner that is rapid and cost-effective.

Managerialism can lead to tensions between target-setting, the drive for cost-effectiveness and the philosophies and ethics of librarianship. Public libraries in the UK are mainly measured in terms of their issue statistics and therefore must tailor a large part of their stock to materials that are in high demand. On the surface this appears to be a sound business response. However, this can cause a tension with public libraries' remit to support learning in the community. A traditional public library philosophy has been to fulfil the role of 'the people's university', but in recent times public libraries have been criticized for failing to develop the breadth and depth of their collections in the race to satisfy mainstream demands (McMenemy, 2007; Christie, 2008). Their approach to stock acquisition has also attracted criticism, when these processes have been contracted out to one major supplier for cost-efficiency reasons. It is believed that this has resulted in the purchase of materials of far less diversity than previously, leading to a neglect of smaller publishing houses and local bookselling businesses. Potentially this affects the quality of books published for all of us as the market adjusts to meet these big customer demands. Ethically, most librarians would shrink from taking actions that are likely to be detrimental to the community and culture of the book trade. Librarians in large organizations are not responsible for all such decisions and pragmatism prevails in the face of managerialism.

The managerial model of school librarian is one where the emphasis is on managing resources and deploying them to meet the organization's needs in an efficient and effective manner. Effectiveness is expressed quantitatively, by value-added and other audit-measurable terms. This emphasizes the management skills of systems analysis, target-setting and evaluation. For the school librarian this will mean counting issues, reservations, catalogue use, student and class visits, and reporting on the size of collections and how they map to the curriculum. The following vignette demonstrates this approach.

Alan was given an extra sum of money to buy materials to support a new module on the Tudors for A-level history. He provided publishers' catalogues for the teachers to select from and then purchased the items. A special subject heading was added to the online library catalogue so that pupils would be able to locate the selected books. Alan also used this heading to track the issue statistics. At the end of the year he produced a short report for the history department, which showed that, in his opinion, too few books had been borrowed in relation to student numbers. As a result the teacher discussed with him ways to increase students' use of the new books.

In this discourse, the library's effectiveness is measured in terms of its system performance. It is about meeting targets rather than the quality of the interaction between librarians, students and teachers. We may find in our schools that we have management targets to achieve but does that reflect the sum total of the school's leadership thinking?

The deputy head responsible for the behaviour improvement programme analysed student data and identified that those students with the highest number of classroom exclusions were also the ones with the weakest literacy levels. In order to improve their engagement with lessons she developed a holistic integration package run by learning mentors. As part of that offer she asked the librarian to develop a reading initiative that would build the students' confidence and allow them to experience success as readers.

Target-setting and number-crunching are tools and not necessarily ends in themselves. Clearly this deputy head's priorities, in the light of the data, are to improve relationships and learning experiences for these students. So do our measurement procedures reflect the aims of an educational organization? Do they reflect our philosophy of librarianship? Are they about teaching and learning as a result of using resources or about the resources themselves? This managerialist discourse might be usefully identified with Kulhthau's concept (1993) of the bibliographic paradigm. This is where information retrieval is analysed from the resources, systems and technology point of view, rather than from a user's perspective.

If 'Alan' in the earlier vignette surveyed the history students to find out why their library usage is low, he might obtain insights that would not surface through study of systems data alone. Such a survey might reveal barriers such as the lack of study space available in the library or a perception of the library not being a welcoming place, or simply that the history teachers never suggest that students use the library. His meeting with the teachers might result in some suggested ways forward but it will not be a solution rooted in evidence that is relevant to the problem.

Good practice often develops as a result of personal learning rather than the study of quantitative data, as seen in the following vignette.

Margaret developed an excellent library programme of activities as part of her school's chosen specialism: performing arts. The range and quality available to students and staff impressed the visiting inspector. Margaret demonstrated that it had taken time to evolve the whole programme and it reflected her own learning gained from a Master's programme that she was following.

It is possible that imposing narrowly defined targets upon 'Margaret' might have stifled her creativity.

We need to consider how much time we spend on activities that fall within the managerialist model and how beneficial these are to teaching and learning. How far does this model support the development of the library's educational role? Kuhlthau's (1993) grid in Appendix 1 allows us to consider some options.

Discourse of technical-rationalism

This discourse characterizes professional activities as a set of competencies that can be broken down into their parts, as a set of skills that can be mastered and where the efficiency of their delivery can be easily measured. Practitioners are accountable for the technical accuracy of their work. The model assumes that professionalism can be systematized as a set of guidelines and protocols. It assumes an equality of delivery and does not make any allowance for the difference that varying levels of experience can make to the performance of a role.

This model of school librarianship is one which places an emphasis on the mechanics of the role: cataloguing, issuing books, display work, sending lists of new books to teachers, organizing author talks and providing user education on how to use the library systems to locate items. This discourse, like managerialism, might be said to sit within Kuhlthau's (1993) bibliographic paradigm, with the librarian's role designated as organizer and locator of resources. The priority is to put the user in contact with the required item and at that point the librarian's responsibility in the process is ended.

Diana delivered an induction lesson to Year 7 students every September. She gave each student a new library ticket and explained the rules of the library, its layout and the procedures for borrowing a book. Students were then given a worksheet to complete that enabled them to practise locating books using the Dewey Decimal Classification.

Some may be attracted by this approach because it offers a clear definition of tasks. Alternatively, the approach may be viewed as reductionist, because it does not acknowledge the intellectual or creative processes that lie behind actions. Some go further in their critique of the technical-rational discourse and view it as a denial of the complexity that fills real-life situations. In this critique, these intangible elements of intellect and creativity are seen as essential parts of the professional expertise needed to lead a successful school library and so this discourse might be dangerously limited. It takes more than a set of technical skills to create a dynamic learning environment in the library that users feel is vibrant and responsive to their needs.

After some years Diana began talking more to other librarians who fed back to her things she had not considered. She realized that students had problems with defining what information they needed and in selecting useful search terms. Discussion with teaching colleagues identified an opportunity to teach research skills as part of subject tasks, so that students would learn in a more meaningful way at the point of need, rather than being expected to remember skills from a stand-alone context.

There is a global drive to break jobs down into their parts and identify these as skills. Around the world and across librarianship, making skills tangible is a powerful paradigm. If they are tangible they are measurable. From an organizational point of view, it makes them manageable. From a professional association's point of view it means acquisition of a new skill is visible and can be rewarded. Continuing professional development is considered an inherent part of professionalism. We believe such development is more than just the acquisition of a new skill; it must also be an enrichment of understanding. New learning that leads to re-conceptualization is the most powerful form of continuing professional development. Many librarians are located in the technical-rationalist discourse. It offers a lot of opportunities, but as we have shown it also has limitations. It is interesting to note that CILIP's current Chartership Framework (CILIP, 2008) involves demonstrating the intellectual aspects as distinct from simply the mechanical skills of the librarian's role

Discourse of social democracy

This discourse places an emphasis on the professional's obligations to society, maintaining justice and equality of access for all. Its characteristics are those of collaborative leadership, shared decision-making, responsibility for processes and their outcomes, where professional judgements are valued.

This model of school librarianship is characterized by the desire to empower access to information for all. This is done in the belief that providing access to information is a step towards alleviating social and economic disadvantage. An emphasis will be placed on designing and marketing the service to appeal to all parts of the school community. This leads quickly to the question of how to focus time and budget. In any school, it will not be possible to meet all of the needs all of the time. So targeting resources to achieve maximum effect is strategically vital. In some schools the librarian does this by putting energy into developing relationships with younger students, believing that this is a foundation for the student's time in the school. Others do it by prioritizing relationships with staff, hoping through work with them to reach many more students.

This discourse resonates with the current inclusion agenda that is promoted by central and local governments, as evidenced by many public and school library activities that seek to involve people from marginalized or disadvantaged groups.

Eliza decided to evaluate the library's Homework Club to find out what was most valued and least valued by its users and also to find out why some students never used it. A series of questionnaires and interviews yielded quantitative and qualitative data, answering not only the research question but revealing some unexpected results, too. This evidence helped to plan future development and secure increased funding. An analysis was also made of the attendance register in terms of age, ethnicity, ability banding and overlap with the special educational needs register. It concluded that the Homework Club appealed to all parts of the school's community and was therefore a successful part of the school's policy on inclusion. This evidence was then included in the school's self-evaluation form for inspection.

Public libraries in the UK are driven by national targets regarding equality and diversity. All current and new initiatives have to be surveyed for impact on equality. In 2009 funding is heavily tied into projects that aim to reach minority groups in the community. If a library authority can get itself written into the local area Children's Plan it will be able to access funds for working with children. This requires activities to be made available for those who are identified as vulnerable children. If the library service can show it affects outcomes for these children, it will then be written into the plan and have access to further funding. Therefore, raising the service's profile is crucial to its own inclusion.

Which comes first, the requirement to meet national targets to ensure service survival or the desire to meet those children's needs? The pragmatic might argue that it does not have to be a choice; it is simply a matter of capitalizing on opportunities that help them realize philosophical and ethical goals for the service. Others feel overwhelmed that they must find solutions to help society solve its social and economic needs as laid out in government targets.

A liberal library philosophy is about the service representing and serving all members of the community. Pressure from national targets will always be the driver behind planning. Currently, the over-riding question is how to reach minority groups, and the reality is that this vision must be achieved with limited time, money and energy. This can lead to tension between service priorities and ethics, between providing for the demands made by the mainstream users and the needs of the minority groups. Can the social democratic librarian be all things to all people or must difficult choices be made?

Provoked by a conference presentation (Clyde, 2004) Chris began to question why there was an absence of teenage fiction involving gay, lesbian, bisexual and transgender characters in her school library. Was this censorship by passive omission or fear of teacher and parent reaction if such items were stocked? A small collection of positive stories were bought and advertised through the school counsellor and personal education teachers. Feedback from students via the counsellor was very positive. Chris now believes it is just as important to provide young people with this material as to give them access to information about contraceptives and other aspects of sex education.

The social democratic discourse might also be characterized as the view that librarians uphold when resisting censorship, whether generated by government, business corporations or individuals. Influenced by this discourse, the school librarian wants to make information accessible. At what point does duty of care towards students lead to censorship? Ethical dilemmas are at the heart of professional judgements. In examining our beliefs and reasons in relation to our role, how far will we defend them or how far will we go in order to realize them?

Student voice and duty of care are Nathan's two greatest influences when making decisions about the library. He often experiences conflict: should he allow his 11-year-old students to borrow only manga books or should he intervene knowing that for some, their reading skills would benefit by reading a more appropriate text? Should he negotiate with the students, setting them targets to improve their reading, offering the latest manga titles to them as a reward? Would this be unethical?

The school librarian of this model acknowledges that each individual's understanding of information will affect their behaviour in a library environment. In educational terms, this points towards the need for a child-centred approach to working with students in the library environment. It might also be characterized by Kuhlthau's (1993) concept of studying library services from the users' perspective. As Kuhlthau points out, the professional role can go beyond providing a clear and well ordered system, to that of mediator and counsellor.

Where does this leave school librarianship in the 21st century?

We are now in an age where universal truths are questioned. New technology allows everyone to generate information and its free availability has dispensed with the need for intermediaries to check content, either at the publication stage or at point of access. Society's view of information is changing and in turn the role of the librarian is being questioned, not least by librarians themselves.

The post-modernist discourse in professionalism is seen as an expression of the uncertainty of roles and identities in this 21st-century age. Post-modernism is a search for new ways of articulating the experience of living in a post-industrial, high-tech era of globalization. Its influence may also be seen as responsible for identifying the other discourses of professionalism already discussed.

Post-modernist interpretations have both positive and negative visions for professionalism. Technology presents opportunities for professionals to create and communicate without boundaries. This can facilitate a revolt from what may be seen as the more oppressive aspects of managerialism and technical-rationalism.

Alex was told by his line manager to count the number of pupils entering the library each lunchtime. Doing this took up time that he could spend helping pupils. Conversations with an online librarian community allowed him to see that his role was being measured only in a technical sense, not accounting for the extra work invested in developing relationships with staff and students. So instead of feeling de-professionalized he opened a conversation with his line manager about the educational aspects of the school library.

Post-modernist interpretations also offer more pessimistic visions of professionalism. Roles are so fragmented and de-professionalized by central control and their subjection to market values that they no longer offer a meaningful personal sense of identity. These issues of professionalism have been much explored in the field of health. Some writers (Stronach et al., 2002) encourage professionals to reflect on their local situation and recognize that a professional identity is a complex entity that cannot be explained by one theory alone. Focus should be placed on the positive features of diversity, creativity and trust. Professionalism is aptly defined as 'judgement in conditions of uncertainty' (Fish and De Cossart, 2006), which reflects the plural nature of our experiences. Decisions, large or small, ethical or otherwise, are made amid the messiness that is real life.

We can develop our own vision of professionalism. We do not

have to adopt or stick to one type of discourse, as to do so may leave one confused, disempowered and de-professionalized. It becomes more important than ever to examine our central values and to be clear about what we see as professional practice. There may be elements of each of these models that we need to meld and bring together into our own vision. We need to be able to set targets, to be aware of skills required but also to move into the creative context. In education the level of change experienced in the past 20 years has been immense and discourse has become a sophisticated tool. Clarity of personal vision enables us to identify when we are being re-positioned by a particular discourse and to engage with it critically in order to achieve personal meaning, whether in agreement or disagreement.

Essential ingredients for success in this dynamic environment are a clear sense of self, vision and ethics. Even those who have been in the profession for some time recognize the need to re-examine values. By revisiting our personal philosophies we can identify the most appropriate course of action. The word professionalism comes from the Latin word 'profiteor', to profess, to make a commitment to a set of values. It is this most intangible aspect that gives professionalism its greatest strength and passion.

What is our view of professionalism in the school library? What should it encompass? If we want to raise our profile we need to develop a vision: on which issues will we not compromise? What is it that we are prepared to fight for? What reflects the core values of our professionalism? That knowledge is the basis of our professionalism.

What influences the school librarian's professional identity?

To be a successful librarian one needs to negotiate with the meaning of professionalism. That can only be done with insight into how others see us and our professional practice and by examining the ways in which others construct our professionalism. Job descriptions are a concrete expression of espoused values and can be used as a trigger for dialogue about our own roles.

At an informal librarians' meeting someone asked Emily what her job description was like. This made Emily revisit the document and she was shocked to see that it no longer matched her ideas of what was important in her job. She looked at the sample job description recommended by CILIP (Barrett and Douglas, 2004) and read about teachers' job descriptions in *What Makes a Good School Now?* (Brighouse, 2008). Having made some notes on different approaches (see below) she asked her line manager what she thought and was shown a teacher's job description which was much more centred on teaching and learning than on competencies. Together they worked on bringing the librarian's job description into line with those of other heads of departments.

Examples of different kinds of job descriptions
Version 1: Job description with a management/ routines focus (technical-rationalism discourse)
Responsible for:

- the organization and day-to-day running of the Library Resources Centre

- the selection, maintenance and exploitation of stock
- financial management including planning and monitoring expenditure
- promoting library use
- promoting literacy skills and reading for pleasure
- delivering information and learning skills in collaboration with teachers
- liaising and co-operating with staff and advising pupils
- evaluating, record keeping and reporting
- managing the library assistant.

Version 2: Job description with a focus on librarianship knowledge and skills (managerial discourse) (Barrett and Douglas, 2004, 94)

- Management of a learning resource centre that contributes to the learning targets of the school, growing in line with educational initiatives
- Participation in school-wide development through the regular cycle of meetings with senior staff
- Generating and implementing the library improvement plan and managing the library budget
- Acting as a co-educator by teaching staff and students information literacy skills within curriculum contexts, particularly collaborating in the design and delivery of resource-based learning experiences
- Acting as an information navigator by selecting appropriate resources in all formats and bridging the gaps between

students and teachers and online/electronic information, the
curriculum and subject teaching
- Developing the library's contribution to literacy programmes
and to inspire and enthuse students to read widely
- Maintaining and developing a working knowledge of
educational initiatives, information and communications
technologies and developments in school librarianship.

Version 3: Job description with a leadership/teaching and learning focus (social-democracy discourse) (using ideas from Brighouse, 2008, 78)

Principle accountabilities:

- ensuring, in consultation with teaching colleagues, that the
library supports curriculum delivery
- taking the lead, in conjunction with teaching colleagues, in
creating a whole-school reading culture and promoting wider
reading and literacy
- supporting, in collaboration with teachers, the development
of pupils as independent and lifelong learners, working with
whole classes and individual learners
- contributing to the Every Child Matters agenda by ensuring
that library provision supports the needs of the whole person
in a safe and secure learning environment
- managing the operation of the library, continually reflecting
on practice so that the service evolves and improves to meet
its users' needs.

The work environment

The work environment, with its intricate rituals and pressures, is a microcosm of its wider society. The social and political realities of our work relationships can present enjoyment, satisfaction, bewilderment, alienation and heartache. The nature of the organization affects our professional identity. In some schools, the librarian is seen as the keeper of books, in others, as someone working at the heart of the learning process. One of the strongest influences will be the lead set by the headteacher; his or her vision of professionalism and how far it permeates the senior leadership team is fundamental to the organization and the librarian's place within it.

Lia's headteacher gave an assembly about his summer reading choices and began by saying he always goes to Ms Kanton in the library for help with his choices because she knows all the latest books and always finds something that really suits him, and this was no exception . . .

This headteacher invested Lia with authority in the minds of his audience. Within a school, everyone will have different views of the librarian as coloured by their previous experiences and the attitudes of those around them.

Our confidence and effectiveness in responding to the range of demands made, develop our professional identity in the eyes of others. So too do our image and appearance. This does not refer to the power-dressing concept of the 1980s, but to group theory. If we want to be part of a group, then we need to adopt their image. If the leaders in our organization dress smartly, then we should do the same to be identified with their values.

Our professional identity

Values and philosophies drive the professional identity we wish
to convey. Where these are unclear to others they may affect the
visibility of our role within the school. This is where a deeper
consideration of group theory can take our understanding to the
next level. Forsyth (2006) describes the stages of Tuckman's
theory of group development as forming, storming, norming,
performing and adjourning. 'Storming' refers to engagement
and intellectual conflict with each other; it is where appreciation
of other viewpoints is gained and jointly understood meanings
are achieved. This process helps provide individuals with
insight into ways forward in order to achieve the group goals.
One cannot reach successful 'performance' without developing
those relationships.

Our understanding of this theory is underlined by the
findings of research into teachers' awareness of information
literacy (Williams and Coles, 2003). Although this understanding was limited at the project outset, after engagement,
teachers understood information literacy to be a useful
consideration. One of the barriers to their understanding was
the librarians' use of linear models. These concepts were
interpreted by teachers as being more about the library than
learning. The research showed that even with understanding,
the teachers felt too overwhelmed by other demands to be able
to take on what they perceived as extra tasks. Williams and
Coles (2003) recommended that librarians continue to engage
with teachers, finding ways to develop student skills and to
express matters in a learning rather than library context.
Tuckman (Forsythe, 2006) emphasizes that some of his stages

are cyclical, so 'storming' may be a continual process for teachers and librarians to explore and negotiate meanings. Our professional role cannot be perceived by teachers unless we engage intellectually with them. Professionalism is about more than wearing similar apparel.

How we are received and treated reinforces our professional identity and, in this context, a concept that is particularly relevant to librarians working in the education sector is that of cognitive authority. This theory (Wilson, 1983) is concerned with how people construct knowledge from their own experience and from the ideas of other people. Cognitive authority is the term applied to a person or source of information that is seen as credible and therefore allowed to have influence over one's thinking. As the previous vignette illustrated, if a colleague who is seen as authoritative by others introduces us as an expert who should be listened to, then they extend their authority to us. This establishes our professional identity and in turn gives us the ability to develop cognitive authority in others.

Previous career experiences bring different qualities to the role and identity. Indeed some believe that the solo librarianship experience, common in schools, can be a grueling one for a young professional. Well developed professional experience may be an advantage in such situations. Reasons for job choice affect our engagement, motivation and development in the post and this is reflected in the development of our professional identity. Whatever our background, the difficulties of this challenging role should not be under-estimated. They can be further complicated if we enter an organization where the predominant view of the librarian's role is at odds with our personal vision. This will be explored further in Chapter 3.

To identify the dominant discourse and to engage with it will lead others to view us as effective in that domain. If our comfort zone lies within the model of technical-rationalism but the school's leadership demands more of the activities associated with the social democratic model, the experience is not going to be an easy one. If the school's expectations are that we will simply stamp books and mind the space then those of us with social democratic leanings will feel unappreciated and become very frustrated.

In reality the successful school librarian moves between all of the models of professionalism discussed, depending on the context of the situation. This is sometimes governed by our workplace and sometimes by our beliefs. Whatever our priority may be, day-to-day mechanics, teaching and learning or nurturing children, it will need to fit the school's vision to be effective. Once we have a grasp of our own model it is time to focus on how others see us. In Chapter 2 the congruence between the two views, or the lack of it, will be examined.

2 How others see us

However we view ourselves as professionals, it is an inescapable fact that we work within a context of other people's perceptions of us and demands on us. If we place ourselves at the centre of those expectations, we can see a series of concentric circles with varying degrees of influence, either directly on our practice or on those who influence us. These expectations may be critical to how we function. We will look at the players in these circles of influence and explore the impact they have on us.

Placing ourselves at the centre is in itself a distortion of reality. The library may not be viewed as central to school life. Consequently, the librarian may be seen as peripheral. Our role could be likened to the governess of Victorian times, neither family nor servant, but stuck somewhere in between. This perception has implications for what we may need to do to achieve our goals. Even where the library is placed physically at the centre or the front of the school building, as is certainly the case in some schools, we need to recognize that this is only part of what being central means. Far more important is the curriculum, both public and hidden, and the extent to which the librarian is included in the planning and delivery of teaching and learning in all its manifestations.

The interactions between different individuals and contexts will each produce a different outcome, which we can influence. If we prioritize the more mechanistic aspects of our role, teachers will be unable to see us as fellow educationalists. So do we need to move away from operating within the technical-rational role, as was advocated by Stenhouse (1975) more than 30 years ago? He envisaged librarians developing into 'consultative tutors' who would be able to support students' independent learning.

Paul was facing the prospect of his library being largely replaced by electronic resources. However, he set out to demonstrate that he could work to the head's educational agenda. This agenda prioritized students' competence and confidence in the electronic environment (linked to employability) and the delivery of personal learning and thinking skills (PLTS) in the classroom. He showed that the library was fundamental to this vision of the school's development by collaborating with teachers, in the classroom and the library, to ensure that students were able to use information in all its formats effectively. He joked to the headteacher that he could in time get rid of the 'room' as long as they never got rid of the information expert.

Paul's case illustrates that although the method of delivery of information may change with technology, the fundamental need for information specialists in schools is in fact more crucial now than ever before.

However, success as a school librarian may be measured in

different ways from different perspectives – that of the school, the librarian, others in the profession and external assessors, such as the Office for Standards in Education, Children's Services and Skills (Ofsted) in the UK. What may be perceived as success by one or more of these players may be seen differently by others. This will be discussed further in Chapter 3. Most importantly, we need to ask who the significant players are in the context in which we find ourselves.

Who are the significant others?

While these 'others' can be looked at in groups, it is important to remember that these groups are not homogenous and the multiplicity of views within each group creates both a problem and an opportunity for us. While some individual players may be indifferent or even hostile to our involvement in the school, others will be willing and even eager to work with us.

Within the school community

Teachers

The theatre of operations for the school librarian is largely defined by the views and decisions of teachers. Our self-perception may be very similar to the academic librarians in a large college or even university, supporting the work of the staff and students. In colleges and universities a significant proportion of many students' time will be spent working independently, which gives a greater opportunity for the librarian to offer relevant services. But in schools, at least at Key

Stages 2, 3 and 4 (ages 7 to 16), students spend their whole timetables in lessons. Accordingly, how we can operate will depend on the views of teachers, whether the headteacher and the senior leadership, the heads of department or the individual classroom teachers. We depend on teachers seeing a role for us in developing the learning of their students and being prepared to work closely with us to develop that role.

The single most important factor leading to effective use of libraries in primary and secondary schools is a positive attitude by teachers (Streatfield and Markless, 1994, 179).

We also need to keep in mind the structures within which teachers operate. These include subject departments, year groups, faculties and cross-curricular groups, as well as different levels within the school hierarchy. We should ask ourselves which are the most significant within our schools. We need to know this in order to know where to focus our efforts.

Line manager

Fundamental to how people see us is the line management of the librarian. This can make a tremendous impact on the role and status of the librarian. If the librarian is line managed within the same structure as the teachers, he or she will be included in academic decision-making. However, if line management is carried out through the administrative structure librarians may be seen as separate from teaching and learning. Being marginalized in this way makes it very difficult for our professional expertise to be seen and fully used as shown by the following vignette.

Jasmine was managed by the bursar and only attended support staff meetings. As the academic staff developed their policies for teaching and learning, she felt increasingly isolated from this aspect of school life. She planned a series of induction lessons for new students about how the library could enhance their independent learning. To her dismay, without consultation, these lessons were delegated to a teacher, who merely described the resources available in the library. Jasmine met her line manager and explained how by attending academic heads of department meetings she could contribute to discussions using her professional knowledge. She explained that she felt she had little to offer support staff meetings since discussions about cleaning rosters and prices in the school shop did not seem relevant to her work. Jasmine hoped that her line manager would help her to make better links with teaching colleagues.

The complexity of such a situation means that outcomes are never simple; the line manager may not have the understanding or authority to alter the position. Indeed, they may not have the inclination to help for political reasons of their own. Dealing with this type of conflict is discussed in Chapter 3.

Fortunately, not all librarians are line managed in this way. The quote below comes from a deputy head and shows a very different attitude to the librarian and his role in the school's decision-making processes:

In summary, our librarian is precise, accurate, efficient and all-encompassing in his approach. This is simply what a good librarian is. However, he is also insightful, creative in his approaches – he often uses phrases like 'let's turn this problem on its head' to find the solution – helpful (even at cost to himself) and never ever allows his personal opinion to colour anything he does. He is at the heart of the school and this is often reflected by his magnetic effect on those pupils who would not normally be expected to be seen in a library.

Is he troublesome? He certainly is!! Due to the fact that he sets extremely high standards for his own work and outcomes, he builds a framework which allows others to meet those high standards and, naturally, expects them to be met. When they are not, he does not accept this and move on; he asks those questions – why did this not happen? What can I do to allow it to happen? How can we make it better? Life is easier without tenacity like that – but of lower quality!

(School Librarians' Network, 2008)

Clearly, the librarian has built this attitude through his own activities; equally clearly, the school has been prepared to accept this gift and exploit it fully.

Students

Students are another significant group whose perceptions affect our role. How they respond to us will affect our services. The fact that much of what we do is delivered straight to them as individuals, rather than mediated through the teachers, may give us value in their eyes, and enable us to have a real impact. However, that impact is seldom articulated by the students, and is difficult to measure. They may even see it as personal to them as individuals rather than as part of the educational process.

Collectively, student opinion can be shaped by actions and attitudes that they see in others around them, especially adults in school and at home. Where teachers recognize us as equals students will follow their lead. When librarians are not respected in this way ambivalence creeps in and students are unsure of our status and authority. For example, if teachers do not assess information skills, students will not see the value of our expertise. At a time when 'student voice' is becoming a significant part of the way a school is judged, we have a real opportunity to access and affect student opinion. How can we most effectively use students' wishes to enhance the service we offer them? How do we gain and build on students' opinions in our schools?

Governors

Governors representing the local community may determine the level of budget and other resources we have to work with depending on how they perceive our role. They are influenced by the attitudes of senior leaders that they meet. If they see the librarian mentioned in an inspection report, featured in the school's self-evaluation form (SEF) or if they themselves are invited to be involved in a librarian's appointment, then their expectations of the role of the librarian may be enhanced. How can we be sure that information about what we are doing and its effectiveness reaches them?

Each school is slightly different in how governors approach their role, so it is necessary to find out how they operate in our individual schools. How are staff represented on the governing body? How can we feed information to either those members of staff or directly to governors? How do we develop their sense of the library's value, particularly in preparation for critical decisions, such as the appointment of a new head?

In each school, it is necessary to decide how important involving the governors is for the service we wish to offer.

Parents

Parents also have a role to play. Many parents who are looking round schools with a view to deciding where to send their children seem genuinely concerned about the service the library can offer. On the other hand, there may be little direct contact between librarian and parent once the child is in the school. The image that the concerned parent may have of an effective library may be quite different from the one librarians have. Can parents directly influence how the school librarian is perceived? Do we even want them to? If we do desire this, how do we achieve it? Do we want them to look at basic issues such as resources and staffing, or do we want to raise their awareness of the services we wish to offer and the educational value we wish to bring to the students?

In our experience, the involvement of parents in the library is expanding. For example, themed events, cross-curricular days and author visits need to be planned to reach out to include parents. Some parents make direct contact and may prompt the librarian to develop such initiatives as homework guidelines.

In each school, it is necessary to decide how important involving the parents is for the service we wish to offer.

Within independent schools, governors and the perceived views of parents may have an even larger role in how the school wishes to present the library. Such schools are businesses as well as educational bodies, and attracting parent customers is crucial to their existence. Those not directly involved in the delivery of education may hark back to their own schooldays to form views on what is important. This can put a greater premium on the traditional image of the library than we might wish: silent, studious, book-dominated.

Frances was appointed as librarian in an independent co-educational boarding school to run a newly refurbished library. The head was very proud of his new facility since it was his last major project before his retirement and he took every opportunity to promote the library to prospective parents. A survey conducted by the school's marketing department confirmed that after a year the library had a significant positive impact on parental choice in a competitive market. However, Frances noticed that student use of the library was declining. She conducted a survey which confirmed her suspicions and suggested to senior management that the stock should be changed and rearranged to reflect better the needs of the pupils, even though this would lead to an obvious change in the rather austere traditional environment. Her request was denied because the senior teachers believed it would detract from what parents would expect to see. Frances made some small changes and eventually an inspection report some years later referred to a well stocked, well managed but poorly used library. This gave her the necessary authority to ask again and this time her suggestions were given serious thought and many were accepted and acted upon.

Here we see how traditional attitudes to the library may be modified by both the changes made by the librarian and outside influences reacting to those changes, which in turn can reinforce the changes made by the librarian.

Outside the school

The independent sector aside, views of significant people in local and central government determine the level of resources we receive, through the overall budgets given to schools, at least in the UK. More importantly, they can make significant differences to how we are perceived within the school and the community, through reports they commission, comments they make and visits to schools with the accompanying profile that brings. External advisers and inspectors may have an influence both on government itself and on the public pressures on government to act in particular ways. National and international research may also influence policy directly or indirectly by feeding into the political discourse. Finally, international reports comparing UK educational achievements with those of other countries may influence the political and educational environments.

There is a very real problem for UK school librarians in the lack of evidence about the impact of their work. This in turn has a negative influence on the willingness of UK politicians to direct scarce resources to us. Research elsewhere, notably in the USA, suggests that there is a direct correlation between academic success and the active presence of well qualified library staff (Scholastic Research Foundation, 2008). The instigator of much of this research, Keith Curry-Lance writes, 'A central finding of this study is the importance of a collaborative approach to information literacy' (Lance, Rodney and Hamilton-Pennell, 2000). We will look further at the issues around collaboration in Chapter 7.

Finally, the perception of the school librarian will be

influenced by the image of the librarian in the public eye. The media image of the librarian remains a dubious one, stuck in a past of buns and twin-sets, fingers to lips and stamping out books. Unfortunately for us, the professional aspects of the public library role are often hidden behind a layer of non-professional library managers and assistants. The 'information' or 'knowledge' society we are supposed to live in, far from enhancing our role as information professionals, often fails to recognize that a plethora of information creates the same need for help as a dearth of information. The apparent availability of information to anyone with an internet connection seems to have convinced many that access has been achieved. In fact, we know that only a tiny percentage of information is freely available on the internet since much is hidden from the general public in academic or commercial databases. How can we show that true access is dependent on accuracy, bias, reliability, comprehensibility and relevance? Is physical access being confused with intellectual access?

The school librarian may not even be clearly perceived by fellow library professionals. Many UK school librarians are appointed during term-time only, so they may not be seen as serious professionals. This part-time image, however false, can have an impact on when, how and even whether librarians consider entering school librarianship. Library schools have a big part to play here through initial library education in the modules they include in their courses, and in how they involve practising professionals in the delivery of courses.

In effect, there is a web of influences, both positive and negative. The various parts of the web have varying levels of importance in different schools and with different teachers. School librarians work within this web and seek to influence it by their actions. What are the key influences on how we are perceived in our schools and beyond? Determining these will allow us to choose where to concentrate our energy to support teaching and learning. Chapter 4 will look further at what we can do to carry this out.

What influences the perceptions of these significant stakeholders?

There is now a great deal of material published by central government to help teachers to teach, and therefore help students to learn, more effectively. An example of this is the Key Stage 3 strategy units *Pedagogy and Practice: teaching and learning in secondary schools* (Department for Education and Skills, 2004), distributed to all state schools in England and Wales. These units outlined a number of teaching models with guidance on how to use them in practice. Unfortunately, as neither the school library nor the school librarian are statutory requirements, there was little or no explicit guidance on how to use the library as a tool for teaching and learning. Although as librarians we may see opportunities for our special skills to be of value to teachers and learners, it was left to teachers to decide what use, if any, they would make of independent and active learning opportunities available in the library.

For many teachers, personal experience, either in the course of their own education or in schools where they have taught, will be the biggest factor in determining their attitude to the school library and librarian. Without a significant personal experience they will have little idea of the difference an effective librarian can make, since little emphasis is put on the role of the librarian in teacher training. This is something of a chicken and egg situation: so long as there is no automatic inclusion of a librarian in the staff of a school, there may seem little point in training teachers to expect support from one in their teaching career. Without that expectation, and the understanding of how to make effective use of a librarian, teachers will be unlikely to push for such inclusion. In our opinion, the problem stems from teachers' lack of understanding of the research process – they get by from day to day, but they were not taught themselves at school or at university how to develop these skills, therefore they do not see a need to teach them to students now. They may complain about issues like plagiarism, or poor coursework, or the fact that students cannot extract the information they need from the web. But they do not see how this can be dealt with (School Librarians' Network, 2008).

The head here does not believe information literacy is an important part of the school curriculum. He thinks it is something people just know about.

These are far from being isolated examples: research into teachers' information skills in 2006 found that: 'Information literacy is an unfamiliar term and concept for many teachers, therefore awareness-raising is required. A lack of awareness leads to teachers being unable to judge their own skills and abilities accurately and also being unaware of the complexity of information tasks they set for pupils' (Conroy, 2006).

Conroy also reports that workshops on information skills

aimed at teachers are largely attended by librarians. She further concludes that:

> The key strategic issue that emerged from the project was the lack of clarity over whose responsibility it is to teach information skills. Although many elements of information literacy are embedded in curriculum requirements, teachers tend to focus on their subject rather than the information processes involved. There was seen to be an assumption that someone else will teach information skills, confirming the findings of Williams and Wavell (2006) who reported that teachers consider information literacy a cross-curriculum skill. One workshop attendee described information literacy as 'the ultimate core skill', but it seems at present no-one is ultimately responsible for its teaching.

Another influence on the attitudes of teachers is the inspection process. People will naturally work to the criteria on which they will be evaluated. Hence, an inspection or (in the UK) the self-evaluation form (SEF) can be very significant. It is easy for us to see that we can feed naturally into the self-evaluation process, as is shown in the Appendix 2. Equally, it is easy to see how the library can be omitted from the SEF by schools with no recognition of the library's value and if we are not careful this will happen. The failure to provide evidence of the library's contribution to learning may impact negatively on how the senior leadership team views us and on how resources are allocated. This is equally true in many independent schools, where their contribution to the public good is crucial to their continued enjoyment of charitable benefit, and the library's ability to demonstrate this will support the overall existence of the school.

School libraries in the UK have had a rather mixed experience of school inspections. Staff carrying out the older, longer inspections frequently spent time inspecting the library, even if the actual report gave little space to it. Those undertaking the more recent short inspections, who have chosen their specific targets prior to visiting, may give far less attention to libraries. This is in spite of the very positive Ofsted survey of school libraries published in 2006 which showed that 'In the most effective primary and secondary schools visited, libraries and well trained specialist librarians had a positive impact on teaching and learning' (Ofsted, 2006).

Disappointingly this report has had little wider impact. Will we ever see an Ofsted inspection that focuses on independent learning and the use the school makes of the library?

The same Ofsted report also underlined the importance of the headteacher in setting the school library context: 'Leadership by supportive and knowledgeable headteachers and senior managers was the most important factor in improving library provision. They recognized how libraries contributed to learning and, wherever possible, they appointed specialist librarians to lead developments'.

The perceptions of headteachers can have an enormous impact on how we are perceived and the role we can play. There is no doubt that the advent of a new headteacher is a nervous time for any school, but there have been sufficient instances of new headteachers simply dismissing the value of the librarian (and even the library) and making it impossible to operate, for the librarian to feel particularly vulnerable. Conversely, a headteacher with a positive view can create a climate of opinion within a school that encourages the involvement of the librarian at all levels of curriculum planning and delivery. To what extent can this belief in the value of the librarian be created by school librarians themselves? Indeed, given the pressures on headteachers' time and energy, is it likely that they will be able to develop this view without the active example of an effective and creative librarian?

Kate had been at her school for many years and had had some success in getting involved in curriculum planning, the delivery of information skills and reader development, though the extent to which this had happened fell short of her intentions. A move to a temporary building as part of the Building Schools for the Future programme had put her into a single classroom with little room for the students. When a new head started with the intention of making learning and raising standards the absolute focus of the school, almost the first thing he did was move the library into a large hall and make it a central feature of the school. Kate was able to work with far more classes than before and information skills took a far higher priority in curriculum planning throughout the school.

Given the pressures on headteachers' time and energy, is it likely that they will be able to develop this view without the active example of an effective and creative librarian. It is perhaps significant that this particular headteacher had never worked in a school without a full-time librarian.

How do school librarians think the stakeholders see them?

The school context is the most important element in shaping the perception and role of the school librarian. The school's priorities, set by governors, the headteacher and the teachers to varying degrees, determine that context, while the teacher perceptions of their role determine the extent to which the library and the librarian are used to serve those priorities.

Each school librarian needs to ask how the different stakeholders discussed above see them. What specifically influences their perceptions, in the particular context? The librarian may think he or she knows in a general way what the school thinks about their role and how they perform it but direct evidence is needed in order to be able to work with and perhaps alter those perceptions.

We have collected evidence from teachers in two schools about the way in which they perceive librarians. This was done through a brief survey of teachers' opinions; some examples follow:

Teacher A: 'A facilitator of access to the written word, increasingly from sources other than books.'

Teacher B: '1. Someone who is able to pin-point a book or something that may be similar when a student is specifically looking to gain knowledge in a certain area
2. Someone who can demonstrate and access the internet to find information
3. Someone who can impart knowledge to staff as to what's

available and work with depts to make sure each have relevant information to their curriculum.'

Teacher C: 'I see a librarian's role in a school as promoting reading within the school, helping students with independent study and organising opportunities for literature enrichment.'

Teacher D: 'My expectations are very basic: I expect the librarians to know where I can find books and assist me in looking for the right genres and titles more quickly.'
(Unpublished survey conducted by Bentley and Feltham in 2008; see Appendix 3 for the survey questions)

While these comments are overwhelmingly positive, they clearly demonstrated a limited view of the contribution the librarian can make.

Each school librarian is in a unique context and must explore the range of views that apply in that context to what they already do and what they could and should aspire to do. Chapter 5 looks in more detail at ways of doing this.

We also asked a large number of librarians on the School Librarians' Network to comment on how they believe they are perceived by their teaching staff:

Librarian A: 'Teachers (and most of the population probably) don't seem in the main to regard the job as a profession. There is always the problem of library staff in public libraries being library assistants who are the ones that deal with the public in the main. It doesn't help form an opinion when they meet a librarian in a school.'

Librarian B: 'Mostly a positive experience – many teachers can see my role is more than stamping books and that research and supporting study skills is also an important factor.'

Librarian C: 'Information literacy has not taken off here except by my pushing things in by the back door, e.g. 10 minutes at the beginning of a lesson, bibliography handouts etc. I asked to do an audit and was refused permission (teachers already overloaded).'

Librarian D: 'Most teachers are pleased but surprised when I support a class [by walking] around the students offering help with using the books or computers. I guess most of them still hold to the general view of my post being administrative, collecting resources and making them available.' (School Librarians' Network, 2008)

These comments will resonate with many of us as a full or partial picture of how we are viewed within schools. If that is the case where there are qualified librarians, how much worse may the situation be in schools that have decided that a school librarian is unnecessary?

The comments also illustrate that others' expectations of a librarian may limit the role, unless the librarian has sufficient tenacity. How do we prevent ourselves from falling short in the creative aspects of the role, simply because these are not expected, so that instead of becoming the heart of the school, as envisaged by educational thinkers such as Michael Marland (1981), we remain at the periphery?

What are the implications of the perceptions of the librarian?

How the librarian is seen has clear implications for what will be straightforward to carry out and achieve, and for what will require greater efforts. It will also affect what is deemed appropriate for the context of the school, the teachers and the students we serve.

The most obvious implication is whether school librarians are employed at all, or whether the school library is seen as vital to a school. We are already seeing the replacement of some libraries by computer suites. Some heads believe that simply giving access to the internet is enough. They ignore the need to educate students in how to use electronic resources, and the need to support and develop students' reading for enjoyment with knowledgeable guidance.

We need to publicize the evidence (Lance, Rodney and Hamilton-Russell, 2000) that students do better with guidance from actively involved librarians. To do this, we need to develop the national evidence of our effectiveness and pool this with international evidence; then we need to find ways of communicating this evidence to the decision-makers in our society.

How we are perceived within the school will determine what we can do in our own situation. Where we are viewed positively, as is the case in many schools, we need to build on this standing and then get the news out in the public arena, so that other schools see the possibilities and decide to exploit their library more actively. Where our standing is less positive or even negative, perhaps because of a change in senior management or the headteacher, we need to look for evidence of impact, either our own past successes or examples from elsewhere, and use it to convince staff within our school that we have a real contribution to make.

Conclusion

Whatever the perceptions, librarians need both to operate within them, by taking them into account in what we do, and beyond them by pushing on the boundaries of others' perceptions to create new areas where we can work and develop our sphere of influence. So long as librarians believe that what we do matters to our students, and that the more we do the more effective and valuable we can be to the students, we are professionally obliged to do the most we can to make ourselves count within the school community and beyond – within the community, because that is where we work, and beyond, so that our effectiveness may have an impact on what other schools expect and demand of their libraries, and employ the librarians who can and do deliver it.

Accordingly, librarians have a responsibility not merely to deliver the best service possible, but also to assess the effectiveness of that service and help build the body of evidence that is needed to demonstrate the crucial importance of that service to the students, the schools and the future. Only thus will we build the deeper understanding of the role of the school librarian and challenge the wider education community to exploit that role.

3 **Bridging the gap**

Cognitive dissonance is a term that describes the experience where someone has to absorb opposing points of view (Festinger, 1957). This can arise for us when our vision differs from those of our school community. What may seem the 'professional pathway' for us may conflict with the school management's long- or short-term plans. When this happens, a dichotomy may arise between beliefs and practice; subsequently we may have to try to reconcile our differing perceptions. This dichotomy between practice and professional beliefs can arise across all sectors of the library world including schools (Roberts, 1992).

Is there always a dichotomy?

A dichotomy may not occur if the school has a clear vision of what it wants and produces a job description in line with that vision. The values and outlook of a school should be evident to the prospective librarian at the staff selection interview, so that candidates can judge for themselves whether a dichotomy is likely to arise and whether they wish to continue with their application. The following vignette illustrates a situation that might appear to invite conflict but where in practice it did not materialize.

Sam, a qualified librarian, had a background in science and seldom read much fiction. She had decided to make a move into education libraries but felt her lack of literary knowledge might prove a drawback. At the interview she realized that although she still had to deal with students studying English literature, this was not the major priority for the organization, a sixth form college that specialized in technology. She was offered and accepted the post. Sam enjoyed her work and the management recognized her strengths in science and felt everyone had gained from her appointment.

If a librarian, with a passion for literature, had tried to introduce schemes for wider reading in Sam's school, this idea might well have met with resistance. There was potential for conflict but none arose as both parties held similar ideas about the role of the library and the librarian.

What level of congruence between our own professional beliefs and our school's requirements should we expect? We often reconcile ourselves to the fact that not everything can be ideal and we will not always be in total sympathy with our employers. Unfortunately, as time goes by, tensions may develop when we are constrained to act against our own values, in order to comply with the school's outlook, and so a gulf between belief and practice may emerge. The cognitive dissonance we experience may cause a gradual change in our beliefs as a result of accommodating the school's required behaviour. If the level of dissonance is too uncomfortable and progress towards a resolution unlikely, then we have to decide whether to move on. Total congruence between beliefs and practice is never likely to be achieved but an acceptable level of compromise can make things workable.

In what circumstances might a dichotomy arise?

Misunderstandings at appointment can lead to disagreements surfacing fairly quickly. Sometimes a potential dichotomy is not recognized because certain assumptions have been made at interview, or the expectations of the role have not been made clear. The following vignettes illustrate how misconceptions can arise on both sides.

A vacancy arose at an independent school for a librarian, reporting to the bursar (finance manager). The previous post-holder had been a dual-qualified teacher librarian, had taught information literacy throughout the school and was a member of the academic staff. Mary had worked previously in public libraries and was offered the position as support staff, which she gladly accepted, midway through the summer term. It was a surprise when in September she was asked to conduct library lessons. She refused, stating that she was appointed to a non-teaching post to run the library and no mention had been made of taking classes. It was not something she wished to do. Mary decided to move to another school after the autumn term.

Elsewhere the dichotomy may not be between the librarian and the school but due to external pressures as seen in the next scenario.

Judith's family circumstances had changed and she decided a spell abroad might give her a fresh start. Judith was appointed as a chartered librarian at an international school in the Middle East. She had many years' experience of running school libraries but nothing had prepared her for the isolation, censorship and restriction to outside information that she encountered. Although her new employers were liberal, the confines imposed by the country in which she was working made it difficult for her to resource the library and engage the students according to her professional values. There was no public library system to help provide resources, few other librarians to consult and she had to contend with websites being banned at national level and censorship of some images.

Here in the UK, could we say that we, too, experience governmental interventions such as the centrally imposed National Curriculum, which put constraints on our professional practice?

In reality, dichotomy between beliefs and practice is most likely to surface when there are changes in the school, for example, a new headteacher or line manager, response to an external inspection, or reduction in funding levels. Libraries can be an easy target for a new leader trying to make an impression, because they tend to be more public than other areas of the school and are visible to parents and governors as well as students and teachers. Hence, we can feel we are the focus for unnecessary change which can cause us unease, tension and insecurity. When 'the goalposts are suddenly moved', and the outlook for the library changes, we may not always view the new circumstances as a welcome challenge. The librarian in the vignette below faced such a dilemma.

Colin was delighted when the new headteacher of a rural comprehensive school announced that he had big plans for the library. To Colin's dismay, it emerged that the headteacher's plan was to turn his space into a classroom and to merge the library with the IT centre. The headteacher suggested that the IT manager rather than the deputy head could be Colin's line manager. He felt that books had 'had their day' and wanted a more modern hi-tech image for his school. Colin was upset at this imposition but did not feel he was able to challenge the situation.

Although it might be easy to sympathize with Colin, if he had seen this move as an opportunity rather than a threat, would he have been able to deal with this change in a more positive way?

External school inspection reports can often be a springboard for improvements and for moving a library forward. However, because inspectors have rarely worked in a school library, they can also breed dichotomy through ignorance. The vignette below exemplifies this.

The inspection report for a small independent boarding school recommended that the library should have a security system to combat stock losses. This had implications for the library budget. Mary the librarian did not see this as a priority when the library was not even fully staffed. She pointed out that she was only employed for five hours a day and that most stock went missing when the library was open and unstaffed. A security system would not resolve this unless a member of staff was present as well. Mary was a well respected member of the school community so the headteacher responded by increasing her hours, which enabled her to develop her involvement with classes. The headteacher thought he would like to see how increased staffing affected stock losses before making a final decision.

In this instance the inspection report led to a fruitful debate within the school. The leadership of the librarian in posing questions about priorities diffused potential conflict. Later in this chapter we return to the subject of resolving such dichotomies.

So far, we have examined some sources of tension that are tangible and specific. Cognitive dissonance is not always a conscious experience. Underlying tensions may build up over time, fed by isolation and insecurity. For example, we may expect to be seen and treated as making an important contribution to teaching and learning but find ourselves regarded as an administrator and 'warehouse manager'. In this situation, our belief about our role may be in conflict with what seems to be required by the school. It is easy to believe that we have no input into the school's decision-making processes and become frustrated or disconsolate.

Graham, a qualified librarian in a small secondary school, was particularly annoyed when he put proposals for author visits forward to his senior leadership team and received little or no response. Finally he spoke to his line manager, one of the deputy headteachers, about his frustration over the lack of support in organizing outside speakers for the students. She explained that they were not keen on such visits due to a previous bad experience and felt that there were not enough controls over what a speaker might say to their students. She felt their duty of care outweighed the unknown value that such a talk might give students. When Graham overcame his shock at this explanation, he realized that for him this represented a form of censorship. If they would not allow authors on to the premises, might certain books be next for exclusion? He felt that to pursue what he considered valuable in encouraging a healthy reading culture would only result in further marginalization by the leadership team. He gave serious consideration to accepting the status quo and simply complying with this ethos, but ultimately the strain placed on his professional beliefs led him to seek new employment.

The lack of dialogue between Graham and his senior leadership team caused a deterioration in this situation. The team's misconceptions about the role of the librarian as a professional led them to dismiss Graham's possible contribution. If, on the other hand, they had given Graham the opportunity to voice his concerns and had shown more respect for his judgement, then Graham might not have felt so victimized and the outcome might have been more positive for everyone. Perhaps Graham could have provided evidence for his views on how to develop a healthy reading culture.

Dichotomy can arise unexpectedly in many situations. It can happen when we see things in a fundamentally different way from others in our community. For example, we may regard ourselves as having an educational role in promoting information literacy but our school wants an administrator to 'keep shop' in their library. We may want to promote the power of written literature but our school may believe the internet is all that is necessary. Our school's senior leadership team might demand a silent, austere study space but we might desire a modern, social library. We may see great potential and have ideas for the development of our library but the funding committee may have other priorities.

Awareness of dichotomy may also come from insights into what is thought to be best practice by others in the world of education. Why do we consider the practice of others, or read a set of standards such as those produced for school libraries by the International Federation of Library Associations (2006) if not to examine our own practice? IFLA's concepts of 'cultural sensitivity' and 'intellectual access' are deeply thought provoking. For instance, how do we balance our duty of care to under-age students against the need to provide information about their health? Is this duty of care a real concept or our way of avoiding provision of material that might be considered controversial?

A thought-provoking article or conference presentation can cause us to examine the principles of our professional philosophy. Intellectually, we may agree to follow a code of ethics but, on close examination of our behaviour, will we find a dichotomy between beliefs and performance? Detecting these divergences and seeking resolution is to understand why we do what we do, and is part of developing a professional identity.

It can be tempting when unavoidable tension arises to bury our own professional values. However, in the long run, this is not necessarily a healthy response for us or our school. Is avoiding confrontation the best way forward?

How can we resolve the dichotomy?

Developing awareness of the world in which we operate, as seen in Chapters 1 and 2, is our first step. Dialogue with the wider profession helps us to examine the experience of dichotomy. This understanding gives us choices for possible resolutions.

Certainly, when we apply for any new job it is advisable to examine the vision the school has for its library and to see how closely this matches our own ideals. We need to ask ourselves 'will I feel valued by this employer?'. At interviews we answer many questions but how many do we ask? It is really important to establish what the post entails and the line management structure by asking searching questions at interview. We must do our homework and not be afraid to say no if we feel uncomfortable. To find ourselves in a job where there is a serious mismatch between personal vision and the school's viewpoint will be frustrating and possibly demoralizing. The employer too should be seeking the best possible match and should not be put off re-advertising if necessary.

Kirsty attended an interview at a boys' independent school along with three other applicants. She was a very experienced, well qualified school librarian. The physical appearance of the library was old-fashioned and during the course of the interview it became apparent that so were the views of the senior leadeship team. Kirsty felt that to make the changes she believed would be needed would require a lot of determination and could well meet with resistance. She knew she would not be content just to adjust to the status quo. Halfway through the interview she expressed concern at her suitability for the job and withdrew her application. The post was subsequently offered to another candidate.

Kirsty was explicitly aware of a potential dichotomy so she was able to make an informed decision.

However, not everyone can afford to worry about whether an organization's view fits in with their professional philosophy before accepting a job. We do not always have the luxury of choice, due to financial or personal circumstances. In taking on a post in the knowledge that there are potential conflicts we must be prepared to adjust our expectations. This is the day-to-day reality for many of us.

That reality, when experienced in what is a very demanding and busy work environment, can be stressful. It is important to keep stress levels manageable, not only for the sake of our personal well-being but also to keep our performance effective. One way to ensure the meeting of these goals is to develop clear communications. How can we be effective in the eyes of an employer if we are not aware of what effectiveness looks like to them? An appraisal system is a useful tool for clarifying work objectives and what that means in terms of day-to-day tasks. It enables expectations to be examined and feedback exchanged. The effectiveness of any organization increases when relationships between staff show high levels of trust. This means that communications need to be open and we and our line managers need to feel listened to and valued. Where this fails to take place dissatisfaction increases and can result in high levels of absence, a larger turnover of staff and an atmosphere of conflict.

It takes confidence to negotiate with this reality and a determination to focus on issues rather than personalities. A useful source of support and strategies for developing good workplace relationships in the UK is ACAS, the Advice,

Conciliation and Arbitration Service (www.acas.org.uk); there are broadly equivalent organizations offering help in resolving conflict in some other countries. Looking at the resources produced by Human Resources and Personnel Management organizations (such as the Chartered Institute of Personnel and Development in the UK; www.cipd.co.uk) may provide models of good practice and access to the language of effective management practices.

We all have to make compromises from time to time and we have to be flexible in order to survive. The big question is when is it acceptable to give way on an issue? When is something so important to our personal vision that it is a fundamental principle not to be compromised? Working as a solo professional, as many school librarians do, can make it particularly hard to make this judgement because there is no one with whom to discuss it. In isolation and under pressure, it is easy to lose a sense of perspective and matters can become very personal. We should remember that senior staff have a duty of care for their team members, and trades union representatives may also be sources of support and advice. Relationships with other librarians in similar positions are more than useful; they are an essential lifeline for support in any difficult situation. Discussion with others who have faced similar difficulties can bring new perspectives and understanding, ideas for ways forward, or indeed simply support in doing what must be done.

Indeed the process may well result in a re-examination of beliefs that are to the benefit of one's professional practice as can be seen in the next vignette.

During a line management review the deputy head challenged the librarian, Fai, to increase the number of reading lessons taking place in the library. At first Fai felt emotionally stung as she considered that she was already running a full programme for Year 7 (11 year olds) and to do the same for Year 8 would seriously cut into timetable space for accommodating information literacy lessons. She felt overwhelmed by the potential increase in workload and annoyed that current efforts and outcomes did not seem to be completely appreciated. She talked things over with a trusted teaching colleague and gradually realized that her own core belief was that reading should be the first priority; without it information literacy could not fully be achieved. So she arranged for all of Year 8 to be timetabled in for regular reading lessons with the clear understanding that these could be flexibly moved to the classroom in order to accommodate subject research bookings.

In the face of her line manager's own educational beliefs, Fai was forced to re-examine her practice. The emotions first experienced were deeply unhappy and uncomfortable ones, but Fai did not over-react to them and instead took time to reflect and absorb what such a change really represented and how it could be managed. Would the line manager ask for reading lessons to be increased if she did not consider them to be of value? Sometimes it is only when we are challenged to move out of our comfort zones that moments of real learning and understanding occur that can be fundamental to how we see our professional role.

We began this chapter by defining what we mean by dichotomy and we have examined various manifestations in school librarianship. Although resolutions of the dichotomy itself are not always possible, the symptoms can be alleviated through deeper understanding of the issues, by careful reflection and perhaps in discussion with others. By learning from, understanding and reflecting on the issues we can articulate our point of view more clearly and enhance our professional practice.

4 Identifying and understanding your community

Throughout this book a key message has emerged: the librarian who is closely identified with the processes of teaching and learning within the school has the power to make the most difference. Understanding our community and the range of opportunities there is crucial if we are to make this a reality. This is not as easy as it might first appear. We recognize that schools occupy a place on a continuum from those where the library is more symbolic than functional to those that are seen by its leadership team as key to raising literacy and attainment levels. Schools are highly complex organizations and political in nature – and things are not always as they appear. Exploring beneath the surface will help us to ascertain the teaching and learning priorities of the school so that we can focus our energies. Ultimately our research informs our management of change and leadership of learning.

How do we define our community?

We have to be clear in our own minds how we see our school community. Since it consists of individuals whose needs are ever changing as they grow and develop, study of these needs enables us to evaluate our own effectiveness in developing the library's role. Our professional ethics require us to ensure that our services are representative and inclusive of all in that community, but in practical terms we have to decide who we think the library is for. Should we buy popular adult fiction for staff holiday reads? Should we buy books in Russian for just one pupil when it is not on the curriculum? Should we lend materials to the local primary school? Should we provide a collection of resources for school governors?

There is also the wider community in terms of parents and governors. Do we see these areas as part of our library's role? In the UK, schools in the independent sector must develop their role of charitable use, and in the state sector schools are under pressure to extend their opening hours and enhance community involvement. Do we need to think about who will be using our services beyond the school walls and if so how do we respond to this responsibility?

The UNESCO/IFLA School Libraries' Manifesto asserts: 'School library services must be provided equally to all members of the school community, regardless of age, race, gender, religion, nationality, language, professional or social status' (International Federation of Library Associations, 2006). Clearly this is a statement about parity of access but we would like to take this one step further and declare that in terms of identifying and understanding one's community for the purpose of teaching and learning it must be done *with regard* to differences. Can we fulfill the whole of this brief? There are many competing demands and often as solo practitioners it is necessary to choose where to focus our energies in order to achieve maximum effect.

Sometimes our view of priorities is not the same as others' in the school and it is common for the interests of different groups clash. Any individual may have different needs at different times and these may shift rapidly in the course of a library visit. The need for a quiet work environment demonstrates this perfectly. When sixth formers (the 16–18 age group), for example, have a deadline to meet they want to be left in peace to get on with their work but as soon as each one of them finishes they may want to use the library as a social space, regardless of their peers who are still working. It is no small challenge to balance all of these demands.

John, the LRC manager at a large co-educational comprehensive, ran an extensive library programme with lessons held frequently in the Resource Centre, which was popular and well used. However, each year in the early summer term parts of the area were used for oral language exams and for silent sixth form study. John observed that neither group of users were making use of the resources, merely taking up space and preventing access to those in need of the books. John found himself making up boxes to be sent to classrooms while trying to maintain silence in the working area. He pointed out the impasse to his line manager and showed him a list of classes that had requested access to the library. As a result the oral exams were relocated and an empty classroom was provided for silent sixth form study the following year.

It can be very difficult when we are striving to put our service at the heart of teaching and learning to find that the library is more highly valued as a nice space for meetings than as a facility for students. We need to ensure that our judgement is not clouded by parochial and territorial feelings but is rooted in what is for the good of our community. Appreciating pressures on such things as space is part of understanding our school and our responses to these will be looked at in the next chapter.

Defining our community will lead us to consider the many special groups with their own particular issues. It is impossible to provide an exhaustive list of possibilities here but Table 4.1 illustrates just how diverse members of our communities are.

Of course, each school is different and that is why we need to explore our own community through research.

What informs the ways we explore our community?

There are many ways to identify and come to understand one's community and the processes we select initially may well reveal which discourse of professionalism is our greatest influence at that time. These discourses are described in Chapter 1.

A *technical-rationalist* approach might involve studying our community through the use of resources. We might make observations during a specific time period, use a questionnaire or gather statistical information from an automated cataloguing system. Reports from these systems can be complex and subdivided for example by time periods, type of resource or resource media, year group, tutor group or class, or gender.

Library user	Some points to consider
Table 4.1 Members of the school library community	
Gifted and talented students	Broadening horizons e.g. displays Wider reading e.g. booklists to prepare for university interviews Cultural events and activities
Students with special educational needs	Guided reading scheme Paired-reading club Audio and visual facilities Computer provision Homework assistance Physical access Intellectual access
Students for whom English is an additional language	Graded reading scheme Foreign language dictionaries Foreign language texts Visual dictionaries Audio and visual facilities
Keen readers/reluctant readers	Wide range of material in differing formats and media Reading clubs
Older students/younger students	Zoning Wide range of material in differing formats and media Appropriate furniture and furnishings Age-appropriate displays
Used by classes of students	Class activities and group work
Leisure users	Activities, games and puzzles Music
Teaching staff/support staff	Staff loans Professional development collections Enquiry service Homework help for children of staff
Parents	Activities and events Loans Enquiry service

These data will enable patterns of borrowing to be discerned. Quantitative methods provide patterns of use but do not necessarily reveal reasons for that behaviour. For instance, counting numbers of books borrowed might identify a class that borrows less than others but it does not reveal whether the students who are borrowing books and other materials are reading them, enjoying them or developing their skills. Neither would the figures alone show whether the class borrowing less is selecting more challenging material. One would have to make a further study, possibly involving carefully designed questionnaires and interview schedules to build an understanding (Gorard, 2001; and Cohen, Manion and Morrison, 2007).

Taking a *social democratic* approach, we could begin with observation and discussion to identify the approaches to learning that are prevalent in the school. We might then decide to use 'assessment for learning' strategies (that is using assessment to support rather than to judge learning) to collect more information. If students use a feedback mechanism, such as a reading log linked to the return of books, they can assess their progress and in turn receive formative assessment from us. We will then have a much fuller picture of their engagement with reading.

The research approach that we adopt will be influenced by how the school sees the library and by the type of information it wants. In turn, a school's attitude to and use of its library will echo the prevalent theories of learning put into practice in the school (Streatfield and Markless, 1994).

Ways of thinking about your learning community

When joining any organization it is important to study its paperwork and printed output to gain an understanding of how it presents itself and its priorities to the outside world. In a UK school, looking over the website, the prospectus and the last inspection report, and – once on the inside – reviewing the school evaluation form, its improvement plans, those of the departments and its policy documents will provide further layers of detail. We need to identify this strategic view of the organization in order to be an effective manager; this approach is examined in more detail in Chapter 5. If we accept that the core activities are teaching and learning and that the librarian who is identified with these is seen as fulfilling a crucial role, then ways to be identified with teaching and learning are vital.

The school's own methods of evaluating itself will provide an understanding of where it considers its strengths and weaknesses to be. Identifying a weakness and developing work to contribute to its improvement is a beginning, and how the school goes about this will demonstrate what type of learning community it is. Hargreaves (2000) helps us to think about the culture of our school so that we can understand our successes and our failures within it. He writes of two cultures, which he labels as fragmented individualism and balkanization. The first is the type of school where everyone operates as individuals with little discussion between colleagues about teaching and learning. Then there is the 'balkanized' culture where colleagues form allegiances to small groups but little communication and co-operation takes place as a whole school. Finally, Hargreaves identifies as 'contrived collegiality' a situation where collaboration is imposed by management, with the mechanisms for its workings dictated rather than negotiated. Many times in this book we have written about the isolation felt by librarians but

Hargreaves helps us to understand that there are schools where teachers also feel that they are working on their own. Appreciating what kind of school culture we find ourselves in will perhaps help us to see where we fit in and where difficulties we thought were ours alone might actually be shared. We might find that collaboration is still just an aspiration for teachers, too (Quinn, 2003).

Furthermore, Wenger's theories (1998) about communities of practice and how we learn from each other are relevant to our considerations. Does the school give regular time at meetings for the sharing of teaching practices? Are training days organized by the senior leadership team in consultation with staff? Wenger defines three characteristics for coherence of learning in a community. Briefly, the first characteristic is engagement that defines the communities that we feel that we belong to. The second characteristic is the negotiation of a joint enterprise, leading to building of mutual understandings. The third characteristic is a shared repertoire, which reflects activities from the mutual engagement. In the space we have here we cannot do justice to the complexity and subtleties of Wenger's theoretical work but consideration of the balance that needs to be achieved between participation and reification is useful for us. In the school libraries context, participation with teachers is to devise learning experiences for students jointly, review their success, and agree conclusions and ways forward. Reification is where such participation is made tangible by inclusion in a subject department's scheme of work.

Reification alone does not ensure a continuing role in teaching and learning for us. It is the participation in those relationships with teachers and students that is key. These relationships are much less tangible than many other library activities and so much harder to measure, but without them the library will not be seen as essential to raising literacy and attainment levels.

What does learning look like in our own institutions?

Within any school there will be a number of different approaches to learning adopted by different departments or even by individual teachers within a department. However, there will also probably be a predominant approach that is obvious in the school's paperwork and in how it talks to the outside world about teaching and learning and about student progress and behaviour.

Where are different departments in our schools in relation to learning and what are the implications for the library? Do we work differently with different departments? Not only do teachers have different approaches to teaching and learning, but the approaches of librarians may differ again, and if so this is bound to influence our vision of what the library can accomplish.

If we really want to understand our school community we have to look beyond the library to find out how learning and teaching are viewed by our teachers and ourselves.

Kathy organized an action research project with an A-level psychology group (17-year-old students). This involved the teacher and herself keeping a log of observations during the lessons, exchanging the logs at the end of each lesson, and discussing their observations. The process allowed Kathy to see each lesson from the perspective of the teacher whose observations were focused on the students' different levels of engagement and their progress in understanding. Kathy immediately realized that her observations were focused on the resources and how they were being used. For her part the teacher commented that Kathy's focus on skills made her realize that she needed to spend some lesson time developing these skills. At the end of the project Kathy concluded that to be effective in supporting teaching and learning she needed to identify students' current levels of understanding and work with them to move forward from where they were. Before her next lesson with the group she studied the students' essays with the teacher, to see how well the students had answered the essay question and what sort of support they needed in order to improve.

The resource focus that Kathy had adopted in her observations was driven by her sense of responsibility for the resources. She was concerned about whether there were enough resources, whether they were at the right level for the students and how the students used them. Should she instead be focusing on the students and whether their understanding was being developed? This experience helped Kathy to develop her awareness of other aspects of learning and of how she might adapt her teaching to work more effectively. She found herself moving away from her behaviourist approach towards the teacher's more constructivist perspective. Instead of transmitting information on how to go about researching a topic and assuming that this was sufficient, she now works closely with the teacher to identify student weaknesses and focuses her teaching strategies to support their learning priorities. This project provided a powerful learning experience for both Kathy and the teacher she was working with. How can we engage in such effective learning within out own schools? Is our school a true 'learning community'?

Neil made a presentation to teaching staff about ways to deal with the 'cut and paste culture' among students. He made the link between homework tasks that fell into the first three levels of Bloom's *Taxonomy of Thinking Skills* (1956) as ones that lent themselves to cut and paste responses. Then he gave examples of tasks that involved the use of judgement and decision-making, which linked to the higher-order thinking skills. One of these was a change from 'Find out about Martin Luther King' to 'Compare Martin Luther King with Malcolm X and say who made the greater achievement to the civil rights movement'. Neil's presentation was well received and a number of staff wanted to discuss ways of using the library for homework with him.

As a result of the sound pedagogic relationships that he had developed with teaching colleagues, Neil had already discussed with them the problems of dealing with student dependency on Google at the expense of reading the information to produce work. By using Bloom to illustrate his points and providing practical solutions to change the homework tasks from passive to active tasks, Neil successfully identified the library with teaching and learning. By highlighting the problem in terms of improving students' analytical skills and underlining the benefits to all of changing, Neil succeeded in demonstrating his understanding of teaching priorities.

In looking at different approaches shown in Table 4.2, it may also be useful to look back to our references to Kuhlthau's work

(1993) in Chapter 1. This should help to identify some implications for how we teach information literacy in school libraries.

Table 4.2 Different approaches to learning (Webb, 2009)		
Behaviourist	Humanistic	Cognitive/Constructivist
Leading to roles of	Leading to roles of	Leading to roles of
Organizer Lecturer Instructor	Adviser Tutor	Counsellor
with a didactic teaching style	with a co-operative style of teaching	with a collaborative style of teaching
Stand-alone induction for information literacy	Embedded across the curriculum information literacy model	Student-centred teaching of information literacy

Most of us will have a favoured approach to teaching and learning as well as a preferred teaching that suits us best and when asked to step outside that mode we will experience some discomfort. To be effective, we have to adapt to whichever role best suits the incoming teacher, class and purpose of the lesson. In considering preferred styles of working we may be able to see why we find it easier to collaborate with some teachers than others. Does our preferred style of working resonate with the prevalent approach to teaching and learning in our school?

Schools adopting a predominantly behavioural approach to teaching and learning will tend to view the library as a store of resources that students may draw on to find facts for their assignments. A school adopting constructivist principles of learning will integrate the library into inquiry-based activities designed to enhance students' thinking skills. A humanist approach will involve the library when students want to use it or to engage them in learning in a different type of environment. These generalizations may help but we must always remember that in each school there will be a number of different approaches operating at the same time and sending out discordant messages to students about learning and about the role of the library in learning.

What does learning look like for the individuals in our own communities?

Theoretical thinking in different fields can provide illumination when we are working to identify and understand our community. For instance Maslow's theory of motivation and human behaviour (1998), although originally published in 1954, remains relevant today and encapsulates some clear messages for us. One way of thinking about the role of the library is to adapt Maslow's hierarchy of needs to thinking about levels of service that the library can offer (Figure 4.1).

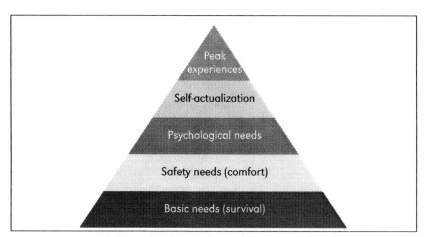

Figure 4.1 Maslow's hierarchy of needs

Maslow believed that to progress from the base to the top of the pyramid achieved a lasting sense of satisfaction. Since meeting basic needs is fundamental to survival, we might think of the library in a physical sense as a place of shelter. A teacher or student might interpret this less dramatically in terms of service, for example responding to their urgent information need with understanding and speed. The second stage could be thought of in terms of nice seating, but perhaps from the user perspective, clear boundaries and a feeling of being welcomed are more crucial to comfort levels. We know from our own experience that we like to be acknowledged; to feel included is very important for our happiness in the workplace. Teachers and students have the same psychological needs; we all struggle with a sense of isolation at times.

If we want people to be good learners, they need the confidence to take risks and we believe that the library plays a key role in all that it does of raising that necessary self-esteem. Peak experiences are the points at which people grow and experience fulfillment. For learners this might be when those 'light bulb moments' occur where a concept suddenly makes sense and the teacher recognizes their breakthrough.

Has the digital environment changed what learning looks like and where it takes place? In the past we could rely on a stable pattern of people walking through the library doors to use resources. Now the emphasis is moving from the library to the librarian. How does the librarian facilitate learning with those who never enter the room?

Eve attended a school library training day led by Chris Powis from Nottingham University. He posed the question 'Who are the Google generation and what do they want from us?' Together the delegates painted a picture of a group with high expectations of computers, who prefer to find out by experimentation or through friends rather than asking for help and who are strategic learners. This made Eve rethink a talk that she gives every year to all Year 11 classes as they embark on a piece of discursive writing for English. Previously she had sat them at the tables and shown them useful paper resources. She did mention some websites but felt that it was more important to demonstrate the books believing the students would never discover them for themselves. This time Eve decided to start her presentation in the students' comfort zone at the computers. She talked them through some key resources, including the library catalogue and online newspaper archive. She found that pupils were much more receptive and many did actually use the books, too, finding them through the computers. Teacher feedback suggested that the quality of work produced was better.

Thinking about the experience of being a learner can lead to unexpected insights into service improvement. An analysis of this coupled with an understanding of how to manage the resulting change and innovation covered in Chapter 8 we believe to be our *raison d'etre*.

An understanding of how our community operates and its cultural ethos requires us to move from superficial concerns to a real insight about how the community works and learns in order to grasp how libraries can best serve it. Inevitably this throws up conflicts and dichotomies; the next chapter will look at ways to respond to these in order to find ways forward.

5 Professionalism and the school librarian

Getting into position

Developing relationships requires energy and that needs to come from us. It takes time to build trust and confidence between people, especially in such a hectic work environment as a school, so persistence is essential. How can librarians respond positively when, as we have seen, others are unlikely to find the time or energy to come to us with ideas? We need to ensure that we position ourselves so that we can capitalize on possible opportunities and this depends on us being alert, proactive and persistent. Our aim should be that in the longer term, when our role is well established in the minds of senior leadership and staff, we will be seen as someone to call on to participate.

Good positioning requires research and awareness on our part. Who are the budget holders in the school? What are the current big projects (e.g. assessment for learning, social inclusion for all, ICT, independent learning)? When we have answered these questions we should consider how we can contribute. If we can go to a project manager with a proposal or solution this will allow us to be identified as someone who is knowledgeable, who participates and can be relied on.

In the first instance, we are our own best resource. We have the expertise and the skills. We should market our wares with shrewdness. Yet even in the most propitious circumstances, things can change and then we need to think about what happens next.

What is possible in the real world of school libraries?

Few schools have all the space they need and many libraries are unable to accommodate the recommended one-tenth of the school's population at any one time (Barrett and Douglas, 2004). Does this mean that we can make no impact on teaching and learning in such a school? Lack of space can be extremely frustrating, yet many librarians fulfil a vital role in spite of this difficulty. Such constraints can bring an innovative response from us as seen in the following vignette.

In a school of 1500, Lynda could only offer seats to 45 students in the library. In the entrance area to the library there was a series of ancient filing cabinets containing a range of resources including newspaper clippings. She surveyed the staff asking them to rank in importance the contents of these cabinets. As a result many of the items were deleted from stock or moved to other parts of the room. The filing cabinets were removed and in their places two small tables and chairs were provided. These were then used by staff and students doing small group work. The staff could see the result of their choices as ones that increased the library's teaching and learning offer.

Lynda succeeded in making the staff feel that their teaching priorities were of first consideration in the library. In the following vignette, teaching and learning are the key drivers in the librarian's decision-making.

The Science Department wanted to book their Year 8 classes (11 year olds) into the library to use resources about renewable energy. Timetable and library space constraints meant that it was not possible to accommodate everyone. So the first class using the library in this way was asked to evaluate the resources and identify the most useful ones for this project. These were then made available as a book box loan and on the virtual learning environment, so that the resources could move to where the learning was taking place in the science laboratories.

The Science Department's teaching has been effectively supported by the librarian and the students have been involved in exercising some higher-order thinking skills. Although not all the classes are able to use the library space directly, a compromise has been achieved that benefits all.

One way to approach library development in a situation fraught with constraints is to do a SWOT analysis. This focuses on the strengths, weaknesses, opportunities and threats that affect the library. The most effective way of doing this is to involve the teachers and students, but we can begin the process on our own (see Appendix 4). This problem-solving approach, particularly when seen through the eyes of others, can lead the librarian to identify new opportunities. It certainly enables us to choose our priorities through the filter of our users' opinions.

It is important to be seen to provide a service not only

physically through the supply of resources, but also intellectually by having a profile in the school as someone who is knowledgeable about educational issues. This should be our area of expertise when working in a school library, just as if we were working in a library specializing in agriculture, we would have to be aware of both agricultural information sources and the current issues in agriculture to be effective when dealing with enquiries.

We can establish ourselves in the eyes of teaching colleagues by giving insights on how current concerns are being dealt with in other schools during conversation and in this way showing ourselves as equally committed and as potential collaborators. This is exactly the process referred to in Chapter 1 where we looked at Tuckman's theory of group development – the storming and norming stages (Forsyth, 2006).

Staying positive

Even though few librarians have generous budgets that cover everything that they could possibly want to purchase, they are still able to make a positive response in difficult circumstances. Some librarians are extremely clever at finding ways to supplement their buying power: negotiating with subject leaders to share costs of purchases, making bids for external grants, lobbying the parent–teacher association and, most importantly, identifying key budgets in the school and demonstrating to the holder how the library can contribute to that area and requesting to be included in the plan. In the following vignette Gary, conscious of his limited ability to buy new books, finds a solution that is not simply about resourcing but is really about harnessing peer recommendation in reader development.

Gary's school library was so small that he could not easily fit in a whole class, so when the head of English said that he wanted to run regular fiction reading lessons, the only solution seemed to be the provision of fiction book boxes. The thought of so many books potentially going missing made Gary hesitate. Finally he suggested that a group of students from each class visit the library and select the books for the box, with a view to persuading their peers to read the choices made. Those students successfully hooked could then return to the library to borrow the book on their ticket. Each successful persuasion would result in points leading to prizes. The English teachers were thrilled with the resulting energy and interest in reading that this peer activity generated.

Establishing a track record with budget holders by providing them with an evidence base is a useful strategy in attracting continuing funding as Marcia demonstrates in the vignette below.

The library in Marcia's school is one of the first places that the head and senior leadership team consider when allocating resources. One of the main reasons is that Marcia is always able to demonstrate a clear audit trail between expenditure and impact on student learning. Projects are always evaluated and reports given to budget holders. Results are expressed both in numbers and in terms of individual student learning. Nothing speaks more powerfully to the head than the students' own voices: 'It has made me read some authors that I would never have thought about reading' (John).

So, is there a point at which a lack of funding makes it impossible for a librarian to make a positive response? This is a question for the individual to answer but clearly there are many librarians with only small bookstocks and few computers who still manage to foster a love of reading and enquiry.

The other major resource that many librarians lack is clerical support. This is needed to maintain adequate opening hours, with supervision throughout the school day, enabling the librarian to do developmental work effectively. In the absence of an assistant, choices about levels of service provision need to be made. Should the running of the issue desk be prioritized over developmental work? Should volunteers be organized to help, or should the library be closed to everyone else while the librarian is engaged with a class or club activity? Is access at all times, regardless of whether or not the library is supervised, the most important thing? Librarians have varying viewpoints because our priorities are determined by our individual professional values. Ultimately choice of service level is determined by the headteacher and the senior leadership team. Their decisions need to be fully informed. Is the senior leadership team aware of the possible alternatives and their implications?

Dale was very upset when told that her library assistant would be required to work part-time on the school's main reception desk. In response she produced a short and unemotive report asking the headteacher to choose one of the following levels of service provision to commence with the change in staffing:

- closure of the library to students and staff at breaktime each day

- only two of the four 'reading challenges' to be maintained
- before-school opening hours to be cut back from 8 a.m. to 8.30 a.m.

Her intention was to reflect the decision for priorities back to the headteacher. By clearly identifying links between staff resources and learning opportunities and without even voicing disagreement with the concept, Dale had subtly outlined the impact of this reduction. Faced with these choices the headteacher decided to organize a different initiative involving student helpers on the main reception desk.

By taking a clear minded management approach to this resourcing problem Dale identified where the responsibility lay and in doing so reduced her own sense of stress at the potential change.

Using evidence to support your case

The task of persuading a senior leadership team that resourcing of the library needs to be increased can be underpinned with research evidence. In the US a series of large-scale statistical studies have been conducted in a number of states from Colorado (Lance, Rodney and Hamilton-Pennell, 2000) to New York (Small et al., 2007). These have found a direct correlation between a well staffed school library and higher test scores for all student grades (Scholastic Research Foundation, 2008).

Benchmarking between school libraries

Benchmarking is another strategy for providing the leadership team or governors with comparative information on which to base decisions about the school library. This form of comparison of data from various school libraries can be used to assess a variety of issues and to underline your chosen area of weakness that requires development. There are different ways to engage with benchmarking. It can be as simple as a list of library budget figures for comparable schools in relation to student roll figures, presented in a grid for ease of comparison. Sometimes this can be quite hard-hitting when the headteacher realizes that his or her peers are actually investing much more heavily in their library. Imagine this presented to show how a larger budget in another school underpinned a successful school-wide reading challenge, resulting in raised literacy levels. The link between student achievement and investment becomes clear. Perhaps acquiring a security system is the goal, then demonstrating the difference it has made in book losses at other schools can be powerful. Accompanying this with a picture of how much of the annual budget is 'walking out the door' never to return each year can provide a strong argument.

Some data will be politically sensitive and not all headteachers will support data sharing in this way. There may well be established guidelines regarding data use so we need to check before embarking on this type of exercise. Indeed, some library colleagues may not be comfortable about their data being made available beyond the conversation. We should remember that we need permission to use evidence that belongs to others.

Alternatively you may like to gain insights by working closely with a neighbouring school library that has features in common with yours (e.g. state of development, type of school, size) to conduct a peer review identifying differences in how a particular problem or service is managed. If considering the amount of fiction borrowed, for example, why is the figure higher in one school than in another? Could it be as simple as the length of opening hours and therefore access, or the size of the budget spent? Or could it be a little deeper as the analysis reveals that one librarian is a regular reader of new children's fiction and the other is not quite so keen? Is it about the nature of the activities promoting reading? What are the differences in their reader development programmes and why are they so? Some factors that make a difference may be outside our influence, but others may cause much thought for reflection. Strategies for acquiring different perspectives are vital for future decision-making because they help us to reduce our sense of parochialism and provide material for reports to our line manager.

Another way of benchmarking is to analyse our service with a published set of benchmark questions such as those published by the UK's Department for Education and Skills (England) for school libraries (Markless and Streatfield, 2004). Standards for school libraries have been published by different professional organizations around the world and provide a framework of best practice for evaluating our own school libraries. An internationally well known model is the UNESCO school libraries manifesto (IFLA, 2006) and recently a new set of standards for the 21st-century learner were published by the American Association of School Libraries (2007). As discussed in Chapter 3, reading about such models provokes reflection and analysis to discern how far one's own library service meets those standards. It is important for us to remember that these represent ideals only, or it is possible to feel overwhelmed by the expectation that this is what should be achieved by school librarians. These inspirational texts do not acknowledge the realism of our own contexts. There may well be good reasons why we cannot meet all of those standards.

Measuring the library service against other libraries and published standards is a useful step in discovering discrepancies and it provokes us to question why and how. To examine actively what has already been done and gain a sense of what is potentially possible is to pursue our goals. We should not base these on assumptions but on critical self-reflection, which we consider to be intrinsic to professionalism.

If we choose to benchmark with a neighbouring school there is one vital ingredient that must be part of the process and that is trust. To measure our service in this way could be a daunting process so a good relationship with the colleagues involved is essential.

Learning from the world

We have said that in the first instance we are our own best resource, but another source of support is working with others – librarian colleagues, teachers and line managers. In addition to activities described previously one can also access library and educational thinking on a global scale through professional organizations and publications. There is a wide gamut of published research on school libraries at our disposal. To read the research of others, even when it was performed in a very different context, can be illuminating. Before undertaking personal research, a literature search of the topic will provide a framework to help stimulate analysis. Findings elsewhere may well agree with our conclusions or reveal why the outcomes are so different within our own context.

By choosing to measure our service against a published model, there is a danger of placing an unrealistic expectation on ourselves. It is worth remembering that such models are idealized representations of a library's potential role; our library sits in the real world, so it will be different. These models present that organization's view and this may or may not harmonize with our vision.

Evidence and narrative can be carefully selected to make the salient points we wish to make to our own school audience. This is an opportunity to use the power of discourse to our advantage!

Sadique understood that the school's financial deficit meant that he might lose the teaching assistant support that made it possible for him to run a really effective Homework Club. So in his winter newsletter to staff and governors the headline article read 'Teaching Assistants are Vital' and the sub-heading ran as '1153 students attended Homework Club in the first half-term this year'. He then relayed in the text feedback from an evaluation of the club's offer and included some direct quotes from the students: 'The best thing is that you can get help.' The chair of governors took the first opportunity available to praise Sadique for providing such an excellent service for the students and made it clear that frontline work of this kind would be a priority for maintenance.

Sadique realized that his evaluation data, particularly the student voice itself, could be used to position the reader to see these staff hours as vital for effective learning.

We believe that it is part of our professional role to dissem-
inate information about what we are doing and struggling with
beyond our own organization and to share thoughts with other
librarians, either informally on email list services or through
professional journals.

Making a difference

So, are we saying that size, money and staffing do not matter?
Of course not. These things do matter a very great deal, but the
most significant resource of all is ourselves. It is possible to
make a difference while experiencing a weakness in one or all of
these areas. The ultimate responsibility lies with the senior
leadership for the level and type of service that they decide to
provide for students and staff. However, it is also possible to use
management techniques, like those mentioned, to make clear to
a headteacher what difference their decisions make to the
service provided by the library. In presenting evidence and
analysis we are fulfilling our role. We are doing the best that we
can for the library and its users.

We have said that we are our own best resource and it is
important to remember that we too have physical limitations.
There is a difference between the nature of our job changing
with new technology (e.g. virtual learning environments) and
new duties being accrued. Many librarians are taking on new
roles – literacy or careers co-ordinators, exam invigilators, or
media resource officers. Some of these roles complement the
librarian's role and provide a useful extension of it; others may

be taken on because there is little choice. Are we taking on roles out of a desperation to be included and seen as valuable? How far might these new roles impact on our librarian role for its benefit or to its detriment? Many of the ideas in this chapter present practical ways to analyse that impact.

Tapping in to school and user priorities

Today the world of education is increasingly driven by targets and government initiatives and these will be reflected in the school's planning and self-evaluation procedures. These targets and initiatives will heavily influence where the school will be directing its resources and energy. Tuning in to these priorities is vital. How can we demonstrate that the library is helping the school to meet its targets? By reflecting the school's priorities in the library's planning and evaluations we are seen as contributing to whole-school objectives. Later analysis of library activities will be identified as useful in building the whole picture of how a school is meeting its targets.

Unfortunately, librarians are not always part of the forward planning process in a school and may not be kept informed as a matter of course. The danger then is that the library's planning and evaluations take place in isolation and are not seen as supporting the organization's shared vision. We must have ways of finding out what is going on. Attending school meetings is essential so that we can be in on the ground floor of what will affect students and teachers. Networking with other librarians and reading the professional literature is sometimes the first source of information about a new initiative. Bringing these insights into the workplace has the added bonus of making us appear knowledgeable about how other schools are implementing new strategies. Contributing such information enriches the decision-making of the school and identifies the librarian as someone who has expertise and experience.

If the library's improvement plan is devised in isolation, the librarian may well be putting forward a vision that nobody else understands or will support. By using the framework established for all middle leaders in a school who must review and set development targets, we identify ourselves to others as a member of that team. We need to question if our development objectives are a personal wish list or rooted in school priorities. We need to ask ourselves if the theme or issue being considered is a priority for the school. We need to find out what conditions an initiative needs for development. We need to understand how it will contribute to teaching and learning.

Evaluating that wish list is a useful exercise to ensure manageability. There is a great deal of literature on school improvement and school effectiveness which can give one valuable insights and techniques for a planning process (Hargreaves and Hopkins, 2005). In Appendix 5 there is an example of a tool that will help analyse a wish list. We need to analyse which of those items are about maintaining an existing activity and which are new or expansions of present practice. We should identify the items about the mechanics of maintaining a library service and remove them from the list because the focus of our plan is to improve teaching and learning.

The headteacher will not want to read about those bread and butter tasks that maintain the library service. However, we do need to have a sense of the time needed for maintenance so that this can be balanced against how many development tasks are put in the plan. If there are too many items in our plan with weak roots and links, the plan will generate little interest from others and make little difference to those whole-school objectives. Activities that are well rooted in wider school practice will be easier to develop because factors exist that will support their development. This analysis will help us to determine a list of priorities that are manageable.

Awareness of school and teacher priorities can save you from wasting time and energy on items that will fail to have an impact. For instance, in the UK context, policy documents such as *Literacy across the curriculum* and *Numeracy across the curriculum* (Department for Education and Employment, 2000; 2001) were not statutory documents, but advisory ones, therefore very much subject to individual school interpretation. On paper, the discourse of these policies was very powerful and persuasive in promotion of particular visions for education, but in reality their implementation was very mixed. Our time and effort spent pursuing those visions in the library is only worthwhile if our school is in agreement with them. Even if policy documents include items relevant to reader development or information literacy that inspire us, it does not guarantee that the school will engage with them and make the link to the library. Such a link is absolutely dependent on how the library and librarian is viewed, as we have seen in Chapter 2.

Schools are expert at buffering away things they only have to pay lip service to and we need to know the difference between those and items that are obligatory. This should be easier in the state (government-supported public schools) sector because these matters are at least published, but may prove more challenging in the independent (private schools) sector.

After 20 years of teaching a content-focused national curriculum in the UK, there is a move towards creating a balance between subject knowledge and learning skills. The new personalized learning and thinking skills curriculum (Department for Children, Schools and Families, 2008) began in 2008. As already observed, where there is room for individual school response, the results for the library are unpredictable so we must investigate that response to enable our planning and practice to be effective. An assessment framework for these skills is planned for 2009–10 by the Qualifications and Curriculum Authority, therefore state school librarians can expect that their teachers will address these changes in some shape or form.

How do we make line-management systems work for us?

Current awareness alone is not the whole answer! We need to build up contacts within school and the obvious person to begin with is the line manager. There is a mixed pattern of line management for school libraries in the UK and this responsibility can range from the headteacher, a deputy headteacher or a subject postholder of some kind, to a teacher, bursar, media resources officer, network manager or administration officer. Line management clearly affects the positioning of the library in the organization. For example, if the library's line manager is at the heart of curriculum development, then logically the library will be drawn in as a tool for those activities. If the line manager is isolated from school decision-making then this may well reflect in the library being isolated from major school development.

Again in the UK, ultimately our actions feed in to formal performance review and this should be a process where the line manager develops a sense of all that you do, regardless of their specialism. At its best, the performance management procedure will offer the librarian a much-needed opportunity to brainstorm problems, find out what's going on in the school and be challenged or inspired by that line manager.

If the library is line managed from a support staff post such as the media resources officer or the bursar this may mean it is identified as a support for resourcing but not actively identified with teaching and learning. This may be agreeable to both school and librarian. Where the librarian sees the library's role as one that is central to teaching and learning, as in the social democratic model outlined in Chapter 1, they may find it difficult to make progress in such work with this type of line manager.

Caroline had been in post at her school for several years and was line managed by the bursar (finance manager). Caroline found it difficult to tap in to the academic life of the school. She became frustrated with constantly having to argue a case for attendance at curriculum meetings. At a professional level she felt she was failing to deliver a service that effectively supported teaching and learning. Caroline's line manager blocked any moves that she deemed as side-stepping her authority. As the politics of the situation became clear and Caroline decided to leave, her post was advertised as administrative rather than academic. Caroline secured a post as librarian in a different school and was given full academic status, reporting to the deputy head.

Line managers can be good and bad; each has their strengths and weaknesses. The headteacher's view of the library is critical to its inclusion in the life of the school but does that make him or her a good line manager for the library? As the following vignette shows it is beneficial if the line manager is senior, part of the academic staff, but essentially supportive of the library's role.

Natalie was line managed by the headteacher and found that he had little time to meet her and develop the work of the library. She put forward a proposal to him, whereby the line management of the library should be circulated among the deputy headteachers every year. Initially, Natalie was very disappointed because the first deputy head to take over the task, although very supportive in their meetings, often failed to follow through on agreed actions. The next deputy head, however, was very clear about their vision of how the library should contribute to the life of a school and supported Natalie's work vigorously at senior leadership level.

Relationships between librarian and line manager need at least to be functional for successful work to take place. In reality, personality always plays a part. A line manager may be well placed to further the role of the library but it should be acknowledged that if the chemistry between those involved is tainted in some way that will also affect success.

The issue of line management versus who can help us achieve our vision is one that requires a pragmatic approach. A hostile line manager can make it impossible to achieve; however, if a line manager is merely apathetic then it is still possible to achieve the vision and find other ways forward. It might be that line management could be considered a matter for administration purposes only. To use a little business jargon, if our activities are part of the deliverables in someone else's area of responsibility other than the library line manager, then it is logical to report those matters directly to them. After all, if an English teacher wished to do a cross-curricular piece of work involving science, he or she would talk to a science colleague. They would not consider being line managed by the head of English as a barrier to working with someone in another department. A pragmatic approach requires one to make judgements about what makes things work and then to pursue those actions.

The principle behind school workforce remodelling in the UK (Rayner and Gunter, 2005) is that all who work with students in the school are to be seen as leaders of learning. We feel this discourse particularly resonates with the role of librarian in an educational institution and is a potentially empowering approach. How we conduct our work and interact with others sets a value in the eyes of students and members of staff. All who work in a school contribute to its overall goal – education. If everyone drives in the same direction, understanding the value of their role and how it contributes, the organization is much more likely to achieve its goal. We believe that to lose sight of that goal is the pathway to marginalization for a librarian.

How do we use other relationships to help us?

It is important to understand how we are seen and many of those options have been examined in Chapter 2. There are some areas in which we must make a positive response:

- as a leader
- as a manager
- by making the most of the line management available to us
- by making good relationships.

Identifying people's areas of responsibility, showing an interest, finding ways to contribute and volunteering for working parties are all ways to exercise influence and build relationships. We can build on all these opportunities to realize our vision of the library's role. For those who operate in the social democratic model as discussed in Chapter 1 it is essential to pursue these options for success. Figures of influence are not necessarily senior postholders; it may be how someone operates that gives them influence over others.

Timing is important. If an external inspection report highlights a need, such as to make greater use of different teaching styles, the librarian can seize an opportunity and focus energy. The opportunity might arise as a conversation with staff to gauge feeling and understanding before deciding how to contribute. Would it be helpful to find the latest material on this topic and supply key people with copies? Doing so would certainly make it look as if the librarian has their finger on the pulse.

A small health warning at this point might be wise – choose your tasks carefully. Too many tasks may lead to feeling over-burdened and possibly unable to manage with all the work that they entail. Action requires initiative to be taken on our part and this may take several forms:

- wait and be told (lowest initiative)

- ask what to do
- recommend, then take resulting action
- act, but advise at once
- act on your own, then routinely report (highest initiative).

(Oncken and Wass, 1999)

Oncken and Wass cleverly identify the behaviours of the wise manager and those of the conventional subordinate. Where would we classify our behaviour in relation to other middle and senior leaders in the school? We need to beware of too many burdens being placed on our shoulders that rightly should sit elsewhere. As Oncken and Wass make clear, good time management is more than prioritizing tasks, it is essentially a matter of identifying the most relevant management behaviour to achieve a necessary goal.

School priorities can be identified and tackled through the established planning and review processes. Decisions and choices about where the library should focus need to be based on evidence derived from any of a variety of evaluation methods. This evidence can also be used to demonstrate the library's contribution to school objectives or to secure support for library needs. We can advance our vision of the library's role by engaging in these processes and crucially by building relationships with others. Collaboration with others and the power of pedagogic partnerships will be covered in Chapter 7.

Learning from the students

In making a positive response, good managers act like leaders by taking the initiative and using the appropriate tools to evaluate, analyse and make decisions. Our relationships with teachers provide an excellent conduit to enable the library to work with students, but we also have our own direct experiences of working with students every day. They too are our current users – so how can we tap in to their priorities?

Openness to ideas is a useful quality in a librarian and as discussed in Chapter 6 ideas can spring from all directions. We are always hearing from our students, but actively listening to their suggestions and reasons can sometimes be eye-opening. Eliciting student voices has become a popular idea. Often this translates as a student council in the school whose focus is frequently on matters to do with the learning environment. The original principle behind capturing and distilling the student voice is to involve students in decisions about the learning process as well as to develop their skills as student researchers (Fielding and Bragg 2003; Rogers and Frost, 2006).

What are the priorities for our students when using the library? A warm, safe place, access to a computer or having someone at hand to help with their homework? Near the end of a lesson in the library we could ask a few students to tell us what has helped them the most and if there is something that could be improved to make it a better lesson next time. In itself this is a source of learning for us and it may well help form some evidence useful in demonstrating the link between the library and learning. Another approach, in the spirit of student as researcher, could involve asking students to interview each other briefly and then report back. Assessment for learning can work both ways.

As we have discussed, what is written in a plan is not

necessarily what the teachers are actually worrying about. What is stated in a policy does not always reflect actual practice. When a librarian sees an opportunity, that door could still be closed by colleagues with different ideas. As librarians, we face these ups and downs every day of our working lives and we have to choose where to place our energies to achieve maximum benefit.

What if our personal vision does not match the library reality?

A divergence between school priorities and personal vision has been discussed in Chapters 1 and 3. If the reality of what is happening in the library does not match school priorities there may well be a serious outcome in terms of performance review with a line manager (at least in the UK). Not fulfilling the obligations of our role in the eyes of others may well result in marginalization. How to resolve these dichotomies has been tackled in Chapter 3.

The reality of what is happening in the library may not match school priorities for very good reasons. A positive response after careful analysis would be to raise the issues for consideration by others in an appropriate school forum. Knowledge of the reality of the library's situation may well provide senior leadership with valuable insights. Think about what steps a good leader would take in the following circumstances: high numbers of students relying on 'cut and paste' in response to poorly designed homework tasks, or the absence of basic research and study skills among sixth formers (16–18 year olds) inhibiting the analytical skills required by A-level studies?

How do we know if we are meeting the needs of our community?

Librarians traditionally collect statistics, particularly issue statistics: how many books borrowed, how many books not returned, how many people through the door and so on. Yet do these numbers really tell us anything important about our performance or do they just reflect a shop-keeper's view of our service? Is a teacher measured by the number of exercise books they give out in a class?

In some schools, figures will show that fewer books are now borrowed, but can we conclude from this that students are reading less? Furthermore, if we inform the English department of the decline in borrowing will it alter their practice? Statistics are only a beginning. It is the voices and the stories behind the numbers that reveal reasons for behaviour. Decisions inspire confidence if they are based on evidence. How far is the library meeting the needs of its users? A combination of statistics and questionnaire and interview data will help provide answers. Reporting on the situation and taking action demonstrates a high level of initiative, professionalism and leadership. Others are more likely to alter their practice if they can see a compelling reason that is core to their practice and goals presented in a report.

Joyce, librarian at a large state comprehensive, was told by the headteacher about an article where a school colour-coded every fiction book according to its recommended age range. Joyce had very strong opinions against any such move, which she saw as restricting access to a free choice of reading. She thought about collecting issues statistics from schools that already did this but felt that she would not be able to draw any conclusions about teaching and learning outcomes from such loan figures. Finally, Joyce took the view that she needed to see the idea from all angles so she undertook a mixture of small-scale research tasks: she offered a questionnaire to all who entered the library in their own time over two days and conducted some small group interviews during lesson time. Joyce produced analysis of the responses in a report for the head. It proposed that in addition to the fiction displayed in an alphabetical sequence there would be six new shelves, one for each year group with specifically recommended books for them. The positive engagement in the research process by students convinced Joyce that they should be involved in the library's decision-making and her actions demonstrated to the headteacher that his interest was valued.

It is important to recognize that it is impossible to tackle the whole range of demands placed on the library all at once. Planning must include the notion of pace. The school librarian's self-evaluation pack produced for schools in England and since applied in some other countries (Markless and Streatfield, 2004) presents a very daunting prospect when taken as a whole but is a very useful tool when used selectively for specific development goals. (See Appendix 6 for an example of how this tool can be used.)

How well are we doing?

Our individual vision and personal standards will determine the answer to these questions. When confronted with an attractive but empty library, one person might take the view that the service is in place and if issues are low and class visits rare this is not the librarian's responsibility. Another would want to know why the library was not used and how things could be changed. Similarly, one librarian with a busy library would happily create graphs for the annual report showing high borrowing figures, while another practitioner would conduct research to show their impact on teaching and learning. In our opinion, this last image is at the very core of what makes a librarian working in the education sector effective.

There are many useful books which tell us how to do the nuts and bolts of library management (Barrett and Douglas, 2004; Bradnock, 2007), but it is experience that develops leadership. Evaluation is more than filling in a form; it can provide a trigger for all that a professional does to enhance their perception and performance. Librarians can influence, lead the learning of others and contribute to change. To make that positive response that characterizes leadership, we must surface above the day-to-day concerns and draw on our excitement and passion, to bring inspiration, innovation and integration to our work.

6 Inspiration

What is inspiration?

Inspiration can be a frightening word to use. It implies passion, creativity, imagination and enthusiasm. To be inspired suggests being endowed with vision and insight, having the confidence to take ideas forward to action and perhaps transforming practice (see, for example, Encarta, 2009; Reynolds, 2008).

People who are inspired brim with excitement and motivation and are prepared to take risks. We believe that most of us have vast potential; we can do extraordinary things if we have the confidence or if we take the risks.

Where does inspiration fit into school librarianship?

Annabel, a qualified librarian in a high-achieving girls' grammar school has a large library with a stock of 15,000 volumes, predominantly less than ten years old. She has had outstanding Ofsted (external inspection) reports praising the use of the library by staff and pupils and the efficiency and professionalism with which she and her assistant run it. However, the library is never mentioned in school publicity and Annabel does not engage in any activity outside the library – not even meeting and talking to other librarians. Annabel feels comfortable in her work and she responds efficiently to requests. As the years pass Annabel continues to be very efficient but finds it increasingly difficult to relate to the younger pupils. The library is still seen as a 'good thing' inside the school but the teachers don't stop to talk or think about it very much.

Caroline has worked in her school library for ten years. She says that she is increasingly conscious of the need to explore new possibilities and find inspiration in order to keep herself fresh and drive the library forward. She wants to ensure that she maintains an identifiable place in her community. She has a well stocked, efficiently run library, which is well used by staff and pupils alike and feels that she has the respect of her colleagues. Caroline enjoys her job but still she constantly looks for more. What drives this? Caroline believes that drawing inspiration from others, inside and outside the school, opens doors, enhances the way she works and provides outlets for creativity. It gives her 'soul food' – enthusiasm and passion that helps generate new ideas and activities, and satisfaction from others being motivated and inspired by her drive. 'This gives me a rationale for my work . . . I believe that inspiration helps to reinforce, clarify and question the vision I have for the library, and if I feel inspired I have a better chance of motivating others to share in this belief.'

These vignettes show two different ways of responding to our professional environment. Annabel is undoubtedly doing a 'good job' and is happy to continue her way of working within the school; Caroline is driven to find new ideas and approaches to inspire her work. Why should we bother to refresh ourselves continually? Does it make us better school librarians? Perhaps part of the answer lies in the nature of our professional context. Schools don't stand still. They adapt to the social environment; they implement waves of curriculum change; they integrate technological advances into teaching and learning; and they work to engage students whose concerns and enthusiasms change. In such an environment we need to challenge ourselves, our conception of our roles and our ways of fulfilling the job of school librarian. We cannot become too comfortable. We need to seek out inspiration.

Many of us feel that we lack the necessary creativity to enable us to come up with great new ideas or initiatives. However, inspiration does not have to come only from within ourselves. We can find illumination in all sorts of places. What is important is that we approach ideas with an open mind. We should be ready to act with an enthusiasm and energy that will enable us to apply those ideas that resonate with us to our own situations.

Having and implementing ideas is not the same as being inspired. Ideas can be safe and low key. They can take your practice forward gradually without disturbing or challenging your views or the views of others in your school. If there are problems you can back-pedal. Ideas are fundamental to good professional practice; being inspired adds an extra spark. It usually leads to risk-taking and demands commitment and passion. Without inspiration we would never initiate fundamental changes in our practice, transform our professional understanding, or fully inhabit our role of school librarian. It is as essential as the air we breathe.

Most of us can recall inspirational teachers; those who stood out because they were quirky or loud or quietly passionate about their subject; those who grabbed and held our attention. These teachers must have taken risks to step away from ordinary practice and no doubt sometimes felt the criticism of their peers. They contrasted with those who knew their subject well and delivered their topics with efficiency, but whose lessons were relatively mundane. Inspiration draws attention, makes people think and will in turn be able to inspire others. Inspiration is a risk worth taking; as Nehru is purported to have said, 'The policy of being too cautious is the greatest risk of all.'

We need determination and courage to take even relatively small risks.

Karen, a librarian in an independent school for 11–18 year olds, had struggled to keep the library silent during study time as instructed by her senior management team. She read an article in a library journal about the 'Mozart Effect' and decided to raise the possibility of playing classical music in the library at a Teaching and Learning Committee meeting. She argued that it might encourage a work ethic and calm the students. Some teachers were openly hostile to her idea but she persisted and was finally able to implement the change for a trial period having carefully chosen the lessons during which she played the music. Her high-profile experiment was successful and some of those who had been sceptical were converted. One teacher even applied the idea in their laboratory practical sessions as a consequence.

When we decide to do something different in the library, we know that we risk distancing ourselves from the view of the majority. Most school librarians already feel that they work in isolation and, although viewed differently from support staff, are not truly accepted as members of the academic staff. Being creative can further upset the stability of our situations but we believe it is a risk worth taking in order to keep ourselves motivated, to inspire others and to improve the library.

Sometimes we hear whispers in school that we are merely 'empire building', 'attention seeking' and 'deliberately stepping outside the box to provoke a reaction'. Change is unsettling for any organization and when it is instigated by an 'outsider' like the school librarian it may cause deeper unrest. To combat this potential unease we can try to ensure that our ideas stand a very good chance of being successful while realizing that this may not happen. Careful management of change can help improve our chances of success. (See Chapter 8 for some ideas about this.)

At what levels can inspiration operate?

Inspiration can be pushed forward on many levels within a school. Options range from 'taking an idea for a walk' with a single member of teaching staff (which may, if successful, then be taken up by others in that department), to going directly to the senior management team with an idea for adoption across the school. It can begin small, based on a personal enthusiasm or an idea for one particular area of practice without a clear view of where it might lead.

Jo, a librarian in an independent school for 13–18 year olds, set up a wiki for her staff book group. She motivated the group members by talking enthusiastically about the potential of this new form of collaboration and encouraged them to think about other applications. One of the book club members, Lynn, also attended regular academic support group meetings with Jo. Two months later, having been reminded about the book club wiki, and discovering that she could create group project pages, Lynn was inspired to set up a similar site for this academic committee. In particular, she could see the value of using this tool as a form of communication between meetings.

It matters not whether being inspired takes the form of a small or large endeavour. We might want to enact sweeping changes or envision one new initiative that is fundamental to achieving the school's goals. Inspiration may also come in the form of an intuition, an insight into why something is the way it is, leading to affirmation of an existing approach or to deeper understanding of the barriers to change. We can control the level of risk and change that we engage with, as long as we continue to seek inspiration and the influx of creativity that accompanies it.

The National Literacy Trust, a UK organization promoting reading and literacy, has a motivational Reading Connects project (National Literacy Trust, 2007), which gives an inspiring vision of what a school that truly embraces reading promotion looks like. The Book Trust provides an audit that schools can use to check how well they are doing. This offers a whole raft of ideas to move the library and school forward. Some librarians will be inspired to use the whole vision and to aim high. Others will take on one of these ideas that catches the imagination, that is new to them, may be challenging within the context of their school, but nevertheless attainable.

For long-term influence and effectiveness perhaps a blend of work at all levels is needed. If we only collaborate with certain individuals our work may become fragmented and we may be viewed as 'unapproachable' by those outside our charmed circle. If we focus our efforts on the school management we may miss the opportunity to make a real impact on individual staff and students in the shorter term. To get a good balance it may be useful to think about inspiration at two levels: the *operational* level (new things to do with students and staff to engage and motivate them); and the *strategic* level (new roles and directions – a whole new vision for the school library that may involve a re-evaluation of our values and how we approach our job).

The operational level

Marianne, a school librarian in a small, mixed, inner-city school, was faced with a large number of students who entered school with low reading ages and with little interest in reading. She had previously tried to engage students in reading by shadowing the Carnegie award for children's literature in the UK. However, she was increasingly worried that the books were not appropriate for her students and that this strategy was having little impact on students' reading. She then read a piece of research that criticized passive activities (such as shadowing big events and arranging author visits) to promote reading (Todd, 2005). This prompted Marianne to find out more about participative events and to talk to librarians at other schools. She was inspired to develop a new and more adventurous reading project with three other local schools: their own book award. This award generated high levels of interest and resulted in Marianne's students reading more widely.

The strategic level

Eric was the librarian in a large, mixed inner-city school. His school was working hard to improve communication with its feeder primary schools. Eric contributed to the 'transitions' programme by giving talks to groups of the ten year olds in the term before they were due to start at his school and by teaching them about the library layout and how to use the online catalogue. Informal discussions with colleagues and with primary school teachers got him thinking more about supporting students' transition between primary and secondary school. He found himself reflecting on one of his fundamental values: that of enabling students' learning. Eric wondered whether teaching catalogue skills and giving information was the best way of enabling these ten year olds to cope when they came to the secondary school. He tried out a number of different strategies including peer teaching, collaborative group work, pairing with older students and facilitating extended activities involving parents and community groups such as a Black History event. Eric found that reconnecting with his belief in enabling learning gave him the impetus to re-invent his practice and not just with the new 11-year-old students in Year 7. He found himself changing the ways in which he interacted with students throughout the school, doing less telling and teaching and more supporting.

How do we keep ourselves inspired?

We can all open ourselves up and be ready for inspiration but where do we find it? In the preceding vignettes the school librarians used colleagues and reading to stay creative. Is this enough? Unlike air, inspiration is not all around us; we must seek it out.

Jane and Philippa, independent secondary school librarians, attended a large information literacy conference and heard a presentation on plagiarism. The dynamism, passion and enthusiasm of the speaker struck a chord; Jane and her colleague realized how little recognition this important issue had been given in their schools to date. Fired with enthusiasm they returned with a resolve to raise the profile of issues surrounding plagiarism in their schools. Jane reported back to her senior management team and suggested a school policy. She also wrote a guide for pupils on how to avoid plagiarism. Philippa also talked to her SMT and suggested that the speaker who inspired this initiative be invited to the school.

Inspiration for us, in our jobs as school librarians, is about professional learning. How do we learn? Formal training and educational qualifications, professional reading materials and networking with each other are tangible ways of learning. At a deeper level it is about us as individual learners. To view professional learning as a matter of acquiring a certain set of skills and knowledge is to take a technical-rational approach. This does not allow for individual differences in development and interpretation, which is the reality in every school library. We can all attend the same course but what we take from it will depend on prior understanding that determines what makes sense to us and what seems compatible with our own library setting. (A list of professional development opportunities in the UK can be found in Appendix 7.)

Real professional learning is a process that is both personal and unique. We make connections between what we already know and the new. We form a deep link to an idea as a result of our professional context, personal values and individual understanding of our role. We then draw the idea in, reshaping it and making it our own. This process enables us to reconceptualize our practice, our views and our philosophy. Many inspirational ideas are sparked through conversations with work colleagues. Discussing topical issues with others can help us make connections and see openings for a different approach to a problem or where to try a new idea. The continuing struggle to make sense of the new, to create new knowledge and understanding, is what drives professional practice.

How does each of us learn most effectively? Do we benefit most from formal study, research, reflecting on models, working with mentors, discussion with colleagues, trial and error, or observation of students, teachers, librarians and others? Perhaps some or all of these are helpful at different times?

However, school librarians are frequently solo practitioners and can become professionally isolated – and isolation can be the enemy of inspiration. Isolation can make all ideas, however good, seem like impossible dreams. It is then easy for the librarian to take refuge in the day-to-day routines that keep us busy, but are not creative or developmental.

So, how do we keep ourselves motivated and full of fresh insights, or in other words, inspired? We may begin by recognizing that inspiration comes in many guises and from many sources; it is sometimes desperately sought and at other times quite unexpected in its arrival.

Inspiration from inside ourselves

Inspiration can be stimulated by critical reflection. However, we need to do more than merely reflect on specific instances of our practice, considering technical questions such as how to 'tweak' a lesson or improve the delivery of a service. This is good professional practice and can be motivating, but is unlikely to inspire. We need to go further and examine our values and assumptions.

Reflecting on what we do is essential to the development of professional judgement, but unless our reflection involves some form of challenge to, and critique of, ourselves and our professional values we tend simply to reinforce existing patterns and tendencies (Tripp, 1993, 12).

Critical reflection will help us to understand and connect with the energy that we need to perform our roles as school librarians. It helps determine priorities for practice and identify sources of inspiration.

Sometimes in the face of difficulties we look to our values for personal inspiration. Our values are deeply rooted; they form part of our identity and underpin our actions. They shape our philosophy and vision for practice. (We have discussed values in some depth in Chapter 1.) However, our values can take a back seat in the face of the everyday demands made on us to keep the school library working. When consciously revisited and repolished our values can be drawn on as a source of strength. A mixture of vision (values translated into practice), enthusiasm and passion leads to inspiration.

> In addition we must believe in ourselves and the potential impact of what we do. We too often undersell the importance and raw power of what we do. We are a noble profession. We don't shelve books, and change toner cartridges – we maintain an infrastructure for social action. We don't reference resources, and catalog artifacts – we teach and inspire . . . librarians can overcome the crushing forces of mediocrity and cynicism – but we must believe that we can. This is what inspires me.   (Lankes, 2009)

However, it is difficult for us to draw continually on our inner strengths for inspiration. We can keep ourselves motivated by asking for feedback, by finding out where we have made a difference, by evaluating our contribution to the school. But, in order to move beyond motivation into inspiration we will often need to look outside ourselves.

Inspiration from inside the school

Sometimes the school itself can provide inspiration through programmes it may already be running or introducing. An inspirational initiative can enthuse us to be imaginative, to develop the ways in which the special resources of the library and our skills can give added value to the school.

An English teacher came to Alice, a school librarian in an inner-city girls' school, with the idea of 'doing something with storytelling'. She had no clear goal in mind, just a desire to motivate the students. Alice and the teacher started to explore the possibilities and their collaboration gave real momentum to the idea. They became more adventurous than either would have been on their own and decided to take students to perform at an international storytelling festival. Alice worked with the students to help them find and develop their stories, gave them opportunities to perform to their peers in the library, and organized their visits to other schools and festivals. The joint initiative became a prizewinning success.

We need to identify and engage with work colleagues who are positive in their attitude and who we can rely on to give moral support and an honest, unbiased opinion. In each school there are people who are active, who have a 'can do' approach to life. Collaborating with them or even talking to them is likely to keep us feeling positive and so more open to inspiration.

> As I go around the country I encounter too many librarians who see the vision, who embrace change, but have grown too tired and discouraged to hope again. They are quieted by the scars of past optimism . . . It may sound simplistic, but for me it comes down to needing some encouragement. We need to know that we are not alone.   (Lankes, 2009).

Inspiration from outside the school

Fellow library professionals can be a good source of inspiration, but this does mean ensuring that we maintain regular, if not frequent, contact with colleagues, even setting up visits to other schools. We also need to maintain a genuinely open and curious mindset and be prepared to be inspired. It is easy to slip into a 'that won't work in my school' mentality, to dismiss different practice because it is in a school context that is not like our own – one with more resources, different types of students, a bigger library or a different curriculum – or even in a non-school environment. We need to develop ways of seeing that enable us to look beyond the surface to the possibilities beneath. The key is not to skip over something written by a law librarian simply because we cannot directly transfer the ideas to our school. We need to stay alert to the possibilities inherent in all situations, to make connections and think laterally.

Susan tries to keep up to date with the professional library press but is also an avid reader of newspapers and listens to radio and television programmes. She admits that a lot of her most inspired ideas are triggered by things that seem on the surface totally irrelevant to school librarianship. She watched two television programmes on redesigning everyday objects using modern engineering principles and techniques. The programme followed two engineers as they redesigned a new toilet and a new brassiere. Neither engineer had any previous experience of designing these objects and so they went 'back to basics'. What they designed was new, functional and exciting. The programmes demonstrated the power of ignoring received wisdom and of challenging assumptions. They made Susan wonder if she took for granted some of the services that she offered and whether she automatically assumed that she should deliver a particular portfolio of activities. These deliberations led Susan to recall a conversation with a science teacher about the most effective balance between laboratory and classroom teaching. She began to question whether she should do all of her teaching in the library and decided to try to find ways of supporting the initial stages of student research in the classroom.

The television programmes had made Susan see the value of questioning all her assumptions. We should also try to learn from colleagues who are inspirational within their own contexts even if these are different from out own. We might examine their values and goals, watch how they achieve their results, and consider which elements we might adapt. We should not be afraid to ask questions so that we understand what influences their decisions and what vision drives their practice. The wider our networks, the more likely we are to chance on some opportunity for inspiration or to hear something that challenges our thinking or our assumptions.

One great advantage we have over some other areas of librarianship is that we are directly involved with learning, perhaps one of the most intrinsically inspiring of human activities. We are concerned with both knowledge and skills, so we can connect with all parts of the curriculum in one form or another, as well as with overarching capabilities such as information literacy and thinking skills. This means that we can look to a wide range of programmes and professionals for inspiration; in the UK these can range from literacy co-ordinators to special educational needs experts, from accelerated reader development protagonists to process-based science curricula.

Assessment for learning was the most talked about topic at school meetings and Lyn's reading of the latest thinking on this subject (Swaffield, 2008) made her review the way she assessed student performance in the library. Swaffield's key message was to identify the learning that you wanted to give value to and then design your assessment accordingly. Lyn's work with Key Stage 3 (ages 11 to 14) readers had been recognized as contributing to raising attainment and she was asked to contribute to the school's new model of assessment reporting. Inspired by Swaffield she seized this opportunity to profile the library's contribution by identifying the behaviours that made a student successful in reading lessons. These included reading in a focused way for at least 20 minutes, working towards reading targets and responding to advice. At the end of term she gave the students a score for each behaviour and a guide on how to improve it. It provided a clear language to use with students in raising their awareness of their own performance. At the end of the following term, Lyn was able to feed back to teachers on students' individual results as well as on the impact of this new assessment of reading behaviours on student progress more generally.

Initial professional education in librarianship provides the bedrock for our everyday practice but it will not keep us inspired. It is ongoing professional learning that provides a wellspring for inspiration. There are many formal opportunities open to the school librarian who wants to continue to learn. Professional bodies offer relevant and interesting courses and workshops both on aspects of librarianship and on facets of teaching; university departments of librarianship and information studies offer accredited programmes; and courses designed for teachers, both in school and out, are often extremely valuable.

Seeing things from the teachers' perspective can be inspirational; it can change the way we think about the role of the library and develop our vision of how it can support teaching and learning. Insight into teachers' values and beliefs may stimulate us to re-examine our own. In addition, new theoretical constructs about learning and how it manifests itself may inspire us to change our approach. As well as learning from the inspirational content of any course we may also learn from the processes encountered. Being a learner in a formal situation can remind us about emotional aspects of learning and enable us to discuss learning with students and teachers in a more focused and informed manner.

Inspiration can emerge from a range of formal learning opportunities but its emergence hinges on how we approach them. An open mind coupled with genuine curiosity is most likely to lead to inspiration.

What has inspired us?

The range of possibilities that we have discussed for obtaining inspiration shows how widely we can cast our nets in our efforts to stay creative, enthusiastic and motivated. This was emphasized when the group of school librarians writing this book stopped to consider what had inspired us to become school librarians and what has kept us inspired in that role.

I was 17 and had secured a place on a teacher-training course when I got a Saturday job at my local public library and was trained and nurtured by the branch librarian. I loved working with the public and, yes, stamping books, but she took me to book selection meetings, out with the housebound service and involved me in running the holiday club as well. She had a clear vision and sense of purpose and was the very model of the 'service ethic'. I wanted to be like her.

I was a good library manager but when I went on a one-day course called The Effective School Library I was changed, in one day, into a more reflective practitioner, something that I had never thought about before. Not only did I learn how to ask questions of myself and about my service but for the first time I began to think that maybe I, too, could do a Master's degree.

My inspiration began with a special needs teacher in junior school who took me out of lessons and, over a space of three years, taught me to read and boosted my confidence immensely by saying that nothing could stop me now and that I just needed to read as many books as possible. I realized a few years ago that life had moved full circle as I now work closely with young people who need help to develop their reading skills. Nothing gives me greater inspiration or satisfaction than seeing them break through those personal barriers.

I was first inspired to become a librarian by my husband's problems in finding the information he needed for a business venture; his difficulties brought home to me the importance of information accessibility, and the idea that I might help to do something about it. Since then I have been repeatedly enthused and inspired by other practitioners and a multitude of training courses. Networking has been a vital part of keeping inspired.

I discovered information science by accident as an alternative to laboratory work and my career has included pharmaceutical market research and financial libraries. Being a school librarian inspires me because of the opportunities it gives for altruism. I love sharing ideas, passing information on to others and watching them learn, develop and create as a result.

Having worked in university, public and government libraries I took a part-time job as a school librarian after a career break. Realizing that I needed to retrain, I seized every opportunity to visit other school libraries. A School Library Association meeting for new school librarians provided the inspiration I needed to embark on a Master's degree in education. School librarianship continues to absorb and inspire me with the various challenges and potential for creativity it presents.

Reality check

We must be careful not to let inspiration turn into frustration, disappointment and ultimately even demoralization, which can happen if we focus on what is unattainable. Before we invest too much energy in a new idea, vision or belief, we should consider our inspiration in the context of the bigger picture – the overall aims of the school and the library. This will determine which ideas are capable of realization and which are not, which can be turned into practical policies and actions or be used as a basis for change.

One librarian who has worked in the same school for ten years told us:

The danger I find is to keep my own ideas relevant to my vision and the organization's vision for the library. I have realized that there is no point in initiating a new practice if it has no bearing on an overall plan but is simply put in place to attract attention. Likewise it is important that the vision I am striving to attain remains achievable. There is nothing more demotivating than chasing after some lost horizon. Inevitably at times there will be brick walls and glass ceilings and although when this occurs I might try to break through the barriers initially, I know I have to remain realistic for my own self-preservation and, at times, agree to back down or try alternative routes. However the crucial point I believe is not to lose inspiration but to nurture it in a variety of ways in order to remain motivated, positive and innovative in my job. It is essential to keep positive.

Inspiring others

School librarians should aim to inspire others. This can appear even more daunting than keeping ourselves inspired. The extent to which it is possible for us to inspire others will depend on the vision, passion and enthusiasm we convey, on the effectiveness with which we carry out our ideas and on the quality of our connections to, and communication with others. It will also depend on the image we have of ourselves and our role in the school. Do we see ourselves in a supporting role or as 'leaders of learning'? Supporters follow others and do not usually inspire. Leaders of learning make things happen. They experiment with practice; they gather and use evidence to make a difference to student learning; they collaborate to influence and encourage change; they model particular approaches (Todd, 2005). 'I think that libraries have tried to support learning, but I don't think libraries have traditionally said 'we want to make learning happen here' (college librarian quoted in Bennett, 2003, 3).

Inspiration also goes beyond networking and sharing experiences – the traditional strengths of the school librarian. It is important to ask who we talk to about our work, our ideas and our values, but we also need to ask how we can enable others to adapt our ideas to suit their own contexts and their own styles, to be inspired enough to grow their own projects.

Thomas's attention was caught by proposals for a professional development day on Web 2.0 for teachers in his school. It was being designed to 'spice up' teaching with wikis, blogs, podcasts and other Web 2.0 tools. He approached the head of IT who was co-ordinating the day and asked whether anything was planned on social bookmarking (for example Delicious) as he thought it helped students to find and organize information. The head of IT admitted that she was not familiar with social bookmarking but liked the possible practical applications of the software. She invited Thomas to demonstrate it to the staff. Thomas felt this was outside his comfort zone as the day was all about teaching strategies used in the classroom. However, he could see the value of contributing to a course that was so central to teachers' concerns. Thomas made sure that he discussed the applications of social bookmarking to teaching and learning with the head of IT before he planned the session as he did not want to give a library-focused demonstration.

People watch what we do more than they listen to what we say. We all need to ask ourselves what aspects of our practice might inspire someone else and how we can build on that.

Does inspiring others mean that we have to be outgoing, to stand out from the crowd, to stick our heads above the parapet? Certainly in some situations we may need to project a passionate and enthusiastic persona. It may be necessary to challenge the status quo, confound expectations and ask difficult questions in order to find an alternative route to achievement or to prod colleagues into change. Some librarians definitely inspire from the front – and enjoy it!

Judith is very conscious of her role in inspiring colleagues. She says:

They have grown to trust me. I give them a lead in how to tackle established views and give them confidence to speak out for themselves. If they see that I can ask questions without retribution but gaining respect, it inspires them to follow my example and ultimately change for the better can be achieved. It is important to become a 'voice' within the workplace community. However, I am aware that what I do, say and promise has to be backed by practical results. I strive to meet deadlines and to deliver what I have agreed so that my colleagues will trust me and believe that I mean action.

However, this approach is not the only one. We can inspire others via the quiet discussion of new ideas, the demonstration of something in action that initially aroused only scepticism, or through a genuine and sustained interest in how our pupils think, feel and learn. Every librarian with vision is capable of inspiring others.

How wide should we spread our net? The most effective librarians do not rely on motivating just one segment of the community. They want to inspire all with whom they are in contact: staff, pupils, parents and other librarians. They believe that through a judicious blending of different methods they can share their vision of the school library and achieve change. Other librarians are less ambitious. They try to inspire individuals and groups, perhaps key stakeholders like the pupils.

Marie, who was already pro-active in promoting reading for pleasure in her school, read an article (Lennon, 2007) by a librarian who had tried to get everyone associated with her school to read the same book, *The Boy in the Striped Pyjamas* by John Boyne. Marie's school was a much larger comprehensive than the one described in the article but she could see that because it would be a real challenge it would also be a real achievement if she initiated a similar project. Not being a very outgoing sort of character she chose quietly to enlist a few key allies among the teachers and held a short meeting to discuss how to get the idea off the ground. So it developed into a group project, which really helped it to take off.

Whichever road we follow, we must remember that inspiring others is not the same as informing them. We need to go beyond imparting ideas, demonstrating practice and merely presenting the evidence. For example, school librarians have spent a great deal of time trying to communicate what we mean by information literacy. In our endeavours to overcome the barrier that language and its meanings pose, we repeatedly design models to show not only teachers but also each other what we mean by information literacy. We use reification, we objectify, and we attempt to make a learning process tangible. We have some success in sharing our ideas. Yet it is in the practice of working closely with a teaching colleague that joint understanding is achieved (Wenger, 1998).

When collaborating we go beyond informing. We begin conscious that we are all in different places in our understanding of a topic, but gradually meanings are negotiated and new learning evolves. Then, at some point, inspiration enters. It is a dynamic process that depends on genuine engagement with other people.

We could be seen as ignoring our own strictures by writing this book, since it informs rather than builds participation, collaboration and shared meanings. However, we believe that in sharing our values and our vision, as well as examples of these in practice, we are taking a positive step forward. We also recognize the need to take this type of communication into other arenas. As individuals we must talk to those entering the profession to promote this specialized area of education librarianship. As individuals and groups we must project our identity and our role within the teaching and learning process into the consciousness of headteachers and future headteachers.

> We need the inspiration and hope to keep us moving forward and improving even in hard times . . . Inspiration is something you have to search for. Don't wait for it, search for it. And when you find it, embrace it, and don't let anyone take it from you . . . Don't underestimate the value of inspiration and do not apologize for becoming profoundly inspired or in inspiring others . . . Inspiration is not everything – you need great ideas, action and hard work too – but genuine learning and growth and real change come to those who are inspired. (Reynolds, 2008)

7 Becoming integral to teaching and learning

We believe that integration is an important goal for the school librarian. (We discussed this in Chapter 5.) In many of the books and articles written on school librarianship, and indeed the whole field of librarianship, integration is presented as the Holy Grail, which implies that we may aspire to but never achieve it. We believe, on the contrary, that becoming integral to teaching and learning within the school is not only a valid aspiration but achievable. In fact it is the process of working together with members of our school community to achieve integration that gives real purpose to our work.

But what does integration mean?

What integration looks like within each specific context may vary but the aim, supporting the core purposes of the organization, must be the same.

Integration is the process whereby the librarian and the functions represented by the librarian become an essential part of the school at all levels. As we have said already, this is part of serving the community in which we work, an essential part of any librarian's role. However, we recognize that integration can occur in a number of different ways depending on context. It involves structure, the internal management of the school and how the library fits with that. It involves social relationships with other people within the school. Above all it involves the place the library occupies within the teaching and learning of the school, its core function, and how we work to be a visible part of the solution to the students' learning needs. (Streatfield and Markless, 1994). We also recognize that this may take place at different levels along a continuum from working with an individual teacher to whole-school involvement. It will also fluctuate over time, as the school's management and personnel change.

Each individual needs to build a vision of what integration looks like in their context, each with a different starting point. There will be a range of possibilities that need to be linked to the librarian's capabilities and aspirations to create a dynamic response to the teaching and learning culture of the school.

How, then do we achieve integration?

Becoming an integral part of the teaching team

As we have emphasized throughout this book, teaching and learning are the core activities of the school and therefore of the library. Where the library is truly successful it becomes so through clearly visible contributions to teaching and learning.

We need to remember that by being seen to serve those core activities, our needs and those of our library will automatically come to have value in the eyes of teachers. Recognition of each other's needs and contributions is an indication that people feel themselves to be a part of the same team.

Support for teaching and learning in the classroom must also be supplemented by support for such student work as extended essays and coursework. We should also look to develop a role as teacher mentors in the field of information literacy and independent learning. These themes may be comparatively unfamiliar to many teachers. In the UK, information literacy skills and strategies have developed a new importance in the National Curriculum in the form of the Personal, Learning and Thinking Skills (PLTS) framework. This framework places new demands on teachers who need to enable students to develop a wide range of skills. However, the curriculum in most countries offers other opportunities for the librarian working towards integration.

The classic mindset behind achieving integration of the school library is to concentrate on bringing the teachers to the library but, as Chapter 5 has shown, it is necessary to reach out in many different ways. We can become fundamental to the work of teachers by helping to meet the teachers' need to provide experiences for students that enable them to learn effectively.

In spite of this need to reach out, it is important to remember that the library is still first and foremost a physical space, housing physical resources. This is a significant part of its function, and will be the main way that it is perceived by teachers and students. We can create value in the eyes of teachers and students by creating an attractive library and by responding to information needs with understanding and speed. Clear boundaries for behaviour and a feeling of being welcomed are crucial to users' comfort levels. We know from our own experience that we like to be acknowledged; to feel included is very important for our happiness in the workplace. Teachers and students have the same psychological needs. We all struggle with a sense of isolation at times. To be good learners, people need the confidence to take risks and we believe that the library plays a key role in all that it does, in raising that necessary self-esteem as well as in providing a safe learning environment.

But being satisfied to stop at this point may lead us to fail to achieve integration. Even at the level of resourcing, we need to go beyond the library walls to enable our community to access resources wherever they are. This may be through a computerized catalogue available throughout the school network or even from anywhere on the internet. It may be by providing subscriptions to online databases. We need to look at what Web 2.0 technology can offer us and our students and teachers, and we will look at this in more detail in Chapter 8.

But without the development of successful pedagogic relationships with teachers and students, we run the real risk of being at the periphery of the main work of teaching and learning in the school. Relationship building is a learning process. An organization's activities and success depends on the strength of its relationships and its people's ability to continue as learners. If you examine what makes a teacher a good teacher it is their ability to make relationships and a continuing desire to find out what works best for learners. If we wish to integrate, then we must be partners in this process. And we must look at our own traditional mindsets as well as those of our community to enable us to tackle this challenge. This requires rethinking, developing a new vocabulary for what we should be doing, and what we want our students to be able to do.

Beyond information skills

Ross Todd (2005b) suggests that we should want students to be able to:

- actively search for meaning and understanding
- construct deep knowledge and deep understanding rather than passively receiving it
- become directly involved and engaged in the discovery of new knowledge rather than collecting facts and data
- encounter alternative perspectives and conflicting ideas so that they are able to transform prior knowledge and experience into deep understandings
- transfer new knowledge and skills to new circumstances
- use a range of complex knowledge construction competencies to transform raw data, prior knowledge and information into deep understanding
- take ownership and responsibility for their ongoing learning and mastery of curriculum content and skills
- contribute to societal well being, the growth of democracy, and the development of a knowledgeable society.

This programme is far more than the perhaps somewhat mechanistic information skills that have been our focus for so long, and that so often still remain undeveloped in our students. Todd's challenge demands that we work with teachers. Information literacy is difficult to deliver without teacher collaboration. The range of abilities and attitudes Todd wrote about can simply not be delivered without our integration into teaching and learning, not as an add-on but from the planning stages at whole-school level. If we accept that these aspirations are valid we need to look at ways to sell them to the school, and offer concrete paths through which they can become more than pious hopes. The ways to do this will vary from school to school. We each need to involve ourselves in how our own schools approach teaching and learning so that we are equipped to integrate our aspirations into those of the school.

Possible starting points

The road to integration needs to start somewhere, and where that starting point is will vary from school to school.

Anna's school has embarked on a programme to transform students' learning and achievement through the 'Habits of Mind' proposed by Arthur L. Costa and Bena Kallick (2000). Careful reading of the programme is enabling Anna to show how integrating her skills and knowledge with those of the teachers can both support the introduction of Habits of Mind and help to develop the attributes of learning outlined by Ross Todd (2005a).

The following vignette illustrates the circle of participation, inclusion, engagement and learning.

The science teachers were very nervous about a new aspect of the GCSE (examination at age 16) course called Science in the News. It required students to research and evaluate resources on topical issues, skills that the teachers knew had not been taught. They felt ill-equipped to deliver this successfully, so they asked Edward whether he had ideas and useful resources. At their next meeting in the discussion Edward demonstrated his understanding of student learning needs and skills and how these might be addressed, which resulted in a jointly devised role-playing lesson based on the enquiry 'Should we be spending more time in the sun?'. This involved students in examining information resources with the librarian to develop their judgments about bias, accuracy, currency and authority as to how this topic is reported in the media.

Interest in enquiry-based learning, and discussions about how the curriculum can be adapted to include this, give us a real opportunity to support teachers in ways that they will value. We also know that information literacy skills, however mechanistic they may sometimes seem, are vital to students. Universities around the world are laying more and more emphasis on the ability to carry out research: 'Universities have welcomed the extended project to be offered as part of A Levels and Diplomas because it gives students the research, critical thinking and evaluation skills they value' (Department for Children, Schools and Families, 2008).

The earlier students acquire these skills the more equipped they will be to meet the demands made on them. It is now up to us to seize this opportunity to integrate our knowledge and expertise to help teachers teach this new extended curriculum. This has the potential to demonstrate the integration of our interests with those of the teachers and the school more generally.

Starting points are just that, opportunities to build relationships and get involved in discussions on teaching and learning. Understanding the curriculum in its broadest sense is vital. In the UK, the centrally imposed National Curriculum, whatever its flaws, has made it much easier to identify what is being taught. In this context, familiarity with the National Curriculum and a knowledge of learning theory make it much easier to build relationships and create a library service that is integral to the life and purposes of the school.

Sustaining integration into teaching and learning

The process of integration needs constant renewal, as teachers and curricula change. Even the most well disposed teacher may slip back into seeing the librarian as an information resource rather than integral to the teaching and learning process.

Olivia was included in the discussions for creating a special curriculum for the bottom set in Year 7, involving theme-based cross-curricular work rather than discrete subject teaching. The head of Year 7 spoke warmly of the contribution she would be making as a knowledgeable source of materials to support the teachers, rather than as a potential co-developer and teaching partner. Olivia could see that this was a good starting point, but that she would need to work hard to develop good quality learning experiences. So she volunteered to help with writing assessment criteria for the skills element of the curriculum and promoted the concept of helping students engage with information in a process of 'mediation' (Williams and Wavell, 2006).

This is an example of high-level partnership with one or more teachers, where the librarian and the teachers work closely to develop a unit of work and teach together as a team. It could so easily have been much less. A school culture which capitalizes on the librarian in this way will be making the best possible use of their investment. As discussed at the outset, where the librarian has been successful in developing and teaching units of work alongside the teachers, that librarian is valued.

Becoming integral to the structure of the school

One of the most important steps the librarian can take is to become included in the academic structures of the school. This is partly a matter of function, to be seen as playing a role in the academic management of the school. The UK libraries professional body CILIP recommends that school librarians are ranked with middle managers as heads of department. For most of us, this is the highest we aspire to. However, in the right circumstances, school librarians may even be included on the senior management team.

Today had a 1½ hour interview with the Deputy Head following some interesting observations of transfer of skills and evidence of problem solving from my year 7 'Learning to learn' lessons to Geography. Also discussed recent inspection of Learning Centre by ICT inspector and District Inspection of School Development Plan – my area of Independent Learning.

This was followed by a request to write one side of A4 on how I would help facilitate whole school development re KS3 initiatives. Received a call from Head late afternoon asking me to join the senior management team!

Still thinking . . . and reeling.   (Pedley, 2001)

This is integration within the school at the highest level. It clearly had to be earned and the context had to be propitious. But any of us may be asked to make presentations to senior management if we can convince the headteacher (or perhaps our line manager) that the areas we are particularly concerned with demand a whole-school approach. The obvious candidate is information literacy, which falls outside the specific responsibilities of any other department, though it requires implementation through most if not all departments.

However, for some of us even integration at the level of middle management is still a goal rather than a reality, and earning it may depend more on the mind set of senior management than our own abilities or contribution. What is clear is that achieving this integration should be our aim, because without it we are excluded from many of the discussions that affect how and to what extent we can contribute to the work of the school, which is the education of the utmost possible of the children entrusted to the school. Whether this is in the heads of department meetings or in a specifically academic group such a teaching and learning committee is not important. The vital thing is to be included in the discussions about the delivery of the school's core aim, since without that presence we may simply be invisible to those planning how to teach the curriculum.

How then can we achieve a presence which is not automatically accorded us? How do we convince senior management that we can make a greater contribution to the work of the school from within middle management than without? We may follow the example of one school librarian who with a mixture of luck and nerve was able to be accepted as a full member of the middle management team.

Jane, a new school librarian, turned up at heads of department meetings – from which her predecessor had been excluded. The deputy head who normally chaired was off that term on sick-leave. He queried her presence on his return, saying he thought she would not find it relevant. When she said that she had found it useful by allowing her to focus library buying on new courses and to build a number of partnerships with department heads, he agreed to her continued attendance.

It is seldom so simple. A librarian already in a school and not in the habit of being included in heads of departments' meetings will probably need to justify attending, by arguing the need to be aware of school curriculum discussions and the school contexts in which the curriculum is delivered. The importance now attached to literacy and independent learning may give further levers. A further lever might be the need to make the library budget as effective as possible; whatever the size of the resource budget, the school will be spending several thousand pounds (or equivalent in other currencies!) on salary costs, which need to be justified in term of service delivery. Inclusion within the academic management structure of the school, with direct access to its academic decision-makers, is a crucial element in enabling us to develop partnerships with teachers. Being line managed through the administrative structure of the school, on the other hand, will put us at one remove from academic discussions and make it more difficult for us to respond to curriculum demands, let alone initiate action to meet curriculum needs.

However, integration within the school goes beyond its management structure. There are other areas to explore that include taking part in or at least attending school events. As already mentioned when we talked of social integration in the school, it is a mistake to see staffing the library as the librarian's main or only duty. We need to mix with teachers in order to be known and trusted by them, and this is as much a priority as being available to students. Being part of school events gives the librarian higher visibility within the school and makes consideration as a full member of the school more likely. There may also be unplanned benefits for our role within teaching and learning, which arise from such participation. A contribution to the school drama production may enable discussion about styles of learning, which illuminate ways that the library may interact with the curriculum. Participation in this way enables the 'storming and norming' stages of Tuckman's process (Forsyth, 2006; as mentioned in Chapter 1) to take place, so it is vital to making us integral to the team.

The social aspect is easily overlooked, but can be a key to building personal contacts with other members of the school staff, and particularly teachers. Taking breaks in the staffroom at the same time as teachers may mean closing the library to students, but it will allow us to become far more aware of staff concerns. Chats by the photocopier may serve a similar purpose – again, it is that necessary team-building stage for developing joint understandings. Each school will have its own habits; it is for us is to discover them and use them to establish a social presence. This presence can then provide additional leverage in developing professional relationships which are all-important in allowing us to serve the school community to the fullest possible extent. But beware, it is important to avoid being sucked into activities such as the school play in preference to spending time on teaching and learning. It is a matter of balance.

Pathways to integration at school level

Actively linking to school priorities will demonstrate where the library can be integral to the school. One example of this is primary school liaison, which is important to most UK schools, and contacting primary schools to offer support either to their libraries or to their literacy programmes can be productive. Year 5 and 6 students (aged 9 and 10) can be invited to visit the secondary school library to take part in activities. Primary school staff might be interested in an exchange of advice on organizing libraries, or there might be more ambitious events that could be planned together.

Miranda suggested to a number of local primary schools that they might take part in a children's literature quiz based on the Kids' Lit Quiz™. She explained that the students in Years 5 and 6 could be organized in teams of four, first at school level and then in an interschool event. She provided the questions on agreed themes. The first year, because of lack of time in the primary schools and on her own part, only one school carried out the school-based round, and the school year ended before the interschool round took place. But it was agreed that the 'trial' at the one school had been very successful, and by starting in September next time and holding the quiz in January after the children had been encouraged to read widely, it would work for all the schools. Miranda also planned to involve the local authority primary adviser, to spread the idea beyond the primary schools in the immediate area. This is particularly important as like many London schools her school draws from a wide area.

Organizing school-based activities, such as author visits and poetry workshops, can be beneficial in raising the profile of the librarian and more importantly increasing the cultural enrichment of students. However, if the aim is integration into teaching and learning, then these visits must be chosen with care. If the activities help contribute to teacher assessment of student progress this will help to produce evidence of impact, which in turn can lead to the library service being seen as integral. Stand–alone activities are not of themselves a force for integration and may even run counter to it.

Some years ago Pat had spotted an offer giving a free Ordnance Survey local area map to each Year 7 pupil. She registered her school but, to her disappointment, over the years it just became an administrative chore for the library with no real benefit. The geography teachers did not even want to bring their classes to the library to receive their maps let alone do any collaboration as a result. So, when the UK government announced the Booked Up scheme, which gave a free reading book to every Year 7 pupil, Pat thought hard about how to make more of this opportunity. She signed up for the scheme and undertook the administration involved. She also talked to the English teachers who allowed her class time to talk about the books on offer so that students could make an informed choice. When the books arrived the English teachers helped to make it a special occasion when they brought their classes to collect them. Some time later a two-day event was held, which celebrated the books through drama workshops.

This is an example of one area where librarians are already involved. Involving teachers and integrating the initiative into teaching and learning may be a step further than we are used to, but will pay dividends in terms of the recognition of the contribution we make.

Cross-curricular activities offer other opportunities – organizing an activity within them emphasizes that we are an integral part of the school's teaching and learning. The whole-school themed day, whether on Black Achievers as part of Black History Month, or on Explorers as part of a day looking at learning styles, is a growing trend within schools and offers real opportunities for library involvement. As these become an established part of curriculum delivery, schools will need to produce evidence of their impact on students' motivation and learning. We should be a part of the team producing that evidence so it is important to seek feedback from both students and teachers. Developing ways to collect data suitable for teacher assessment will become an increasingly important part of our work.

Social bookmarking, through such services as Delicious, is a Web 2.0 development that can allow us to demonstrate our ability to support teaching and learning. The development of Web 2.0 offers us new ways to integrate. Some librarians have taken on the organization of their school's virtual learning environment (VLE). By developing activities for students that make use of the VLE we can underline the learning potential of the library. But to achieve integration we need to go beyond a 'Library' page to embedding the library throughout the VLE, such as linking to the OPAC from every department page, showing relevant library and external resources, advice on bibliographies, citation, plagiarism and reminders about information literacy.

As Ross Todd has said, 'we need to focus on three things: connections, not collections; actions, not positions; and evidence, not advocacy' (Todd, 2001). Therefore, on the foundation of inspiration and the building of integration we now move the focus to innovation, for without it we cannot continue to evolve.

8 Innovation

To innovate means to take risks. Paradoxically this may happen most easily when people work in a safe and secure environment, one that encourages them to experiment and take risks in order to turn problems into opportunities. As librarians, many of us do not find ourselves in such a supportive situation, so why should we bother to invest energy, enthusiasm and hard work into something that might fail?

We may prefer to maintain the status quo rather than bring upon ourselves any extra stress but, as we saw in Chapter 1, as professionals we should continually look for ways to improve our services. Just as businesses cannot afford to stand still but need to introduce new ideas and technologies to keep ahead of their competitors, so the school library should not stand still in the world of educational change and development. Furthermore, we all need intellectual stimulation to sustain our interest, and innovations are a good way to keep us motivated and fresh.

Ross Todd, as quoted at the end of Chapter 7 (Todd, 2001), exhorts the school librarian to reconceptualize the role of the

library, which will inevitably turn the library from an information place into a knowledge-making space. Therefore, using
his three principles, connections, actions and evidence, we will
explore innovative practice for school librarians.

Connect

The pathways to innovation may open up to us through the
contacts and relationships we make in our school, professional or
wider communities. For instance, we may look at the leaders in
our field and ask ourselves what is special about the librarians
whom we admire. We can gain our own inspiration and insight
from seeing how well they innovate and re-invent their roles
(Taylor and Guiney, 2008); prizes for achievement such as the
School Librarian of the Year Award in the UK help to draw
attention to good practice (see School Library Association
website, listed under 'Websites cited' on page 166). It really does
not matter which model of professional practice we choose to
follow as long as we continue to develop our ideas. The vignette
below explains how it is possible to be innovative without
necessarily being an extrovert.

Sean was chair of his local librarians' group. At a meeting there was
discussion about raising profiles and professionalism, which evoked a lively
debate. Sean told the group that although he had been elected as chair of
their committee he did not participate greatly in meetings, often leaving the
discussion to others. Similarly he explained that at his school he attended
meetings and training courses but nearly always took a back seat. When he
had a new idea he would often use a colleague to promote it rather than

himself as he did not feel comfortable with this aspect of his job. He socialized and often helped keep score at sports events or worked backstage for a drama production. His community accepted his persona and recognized the fact that he was well read and up to date with educational issues. Sean liked to see his innovations working in practice as he felt he was giving a valued service. Although on the face of it Sean might not have appeared an innovative person, his skills as a listener and quiet practitioner of his profession gave him an authority and he was held in high regard by his school and librarian communities.

So as we can see, it is not always about leading from the front but we can adopt an approach which suits our personality to achieve the same ends.

Often innovation comes from being 'inspired' by conversations with other librarians or reading about a new initiative and realizing that it could be applied to 'my situation'. It can also spring from a chance conversation with a teaching colleague. In these small-scale cases the new idea may just 'happen' and no formal planning takes place, as Richard's case illustrates.

Richard had worked in a large state secondary school for three years and was aware that 'reading' was coming to the top of the agenda for the English department. Some aspects of current practice had been increasingly frustrating him and so he wrote a brief discussion paper. Using data from the library's computer system he gave statistics showing how little fiction some classes were borrowing. He then put forward some ideas of his own about how reading could be encouraged. For example, he quoted authoritative sources to back his argument that narrative non-fiction such as biography should be approved reading for pleasure in English classes. He was surprised to find that his paper stimulated a productive discussion at an English department meeting and as a result he was invited to hold 'reading surgeries' during English lessons to give personal advice and recommend titles to individuals.

Richard shows that innovation can require us to raise our heads above the parapet. It is more than making small changes at grass-roots level and involves us thinking strategically in order to manage the ensuing change. The networks and connections we form within our communities enable us to take this risk and to act on our ideas.

Act

In Chapter 1 we discussed different models of professional practice. These illustrate the importance of not working in a static environment and show how we need to move with the times in order to gain respect and status. Some of us may feel uncomfortable with the idea of stepping over the safe boundaries of our day-to-day work, so is innovation important for everyone? The crucial factor is that we continue to evolve our role according to the changes and movement in our working environment. This will involve a degree of innovation, including the introduction and trialling of new ideas.

Continuing to develop our professional practice has long been recognized as a key feature of leadership (Roberts and Rowley, 2008). Having confidence to implement our ideas is of utmost importance, and can be rewarding in terms of gaining a sense of personal achievement. Innovation should not be seen as threatening but 'can and should be interesting and exciting' (Newton and Tarrant, 1992). Taking just small steps to introduce a new initiative can be very satisfying and may help to increase interest in the library and raise the status of the librarian and the library.

However, even if we are committed to innovation it can still seem very daunting to implement. Using planning tools may help us take positive action and drive innovation forward, especially if some people are likely to disagree with our proposal.

A good way to begin is to consider these reflective questions:

• What do we want to do?
• Who will benefit?
• Who can we involve?
• How can we make it happen?
• Where will the time and resources come from?
• What difference will it make?

Other tools will become useful at different points in the process. A SWOT analysis is one such tool (see example in Appendix 8). Andrew successfully adopted this approach to move his library forward.

Andrew was appointed by a forward-thinking headteacher to modernize the school library by amalgamating the two existing separate libraries and creating a learning resources centre for the whole school. He used the year between his arrival and the rebuild to prove his usefulness in fiction lessons and to earn the professional respect of the teachers. As part of his campaign to put over his vision he completed a SWOT analysis, which he showed to key members of staff to demonstrate what he felt was wrong with the current situation and how the opportunity of the rebuild could be used to great benefit. Not all staff shared his vision. In particular, some English teachers were accustomed to using the fiction library as a classroom for sustained silent reading. They could only see what they would lose with a library that they would have to share with other classes and individuals. In the end though, Andrew went ahead and won them over as his ideas were realized and they saw the new facilities in action. This he was able to do because his authority came from above.

However, Information Management Associates (2004) suggest that the SWOT method is more of a review tool and they recommend a 'force field analysis', which they say is more useful when trying to introduce a major change. A force field analysis worksheet (Mind Tools, 2008) can help to weigh the pros and cons of a situation.

Whole-school policy-making and planning procedures are also sometimes helpful with developing an innovation but they should be used with caution. They can have the opposite effect and simply maintain the status quo by inhibiting innovation rather than encouraging a critical, developmental eye. On the other hand, at its best, a planning conversation with a line manager can push us to stretch ourselves, be daring and achieve beyond our safety zone. Frances, in the vignette below, shows how such a strategy can be implemented with a positive outcome.

Each year Frances produced an improvement plan, which she sent to her line manager and heard no more about. Then a new line manager was appointed and the school's planning procedures were made more rigorous. A meeting was held where Frances presented her draft improvement plan and explained her hopes and difficulties. She found it so empowering to have someone to exchange ideas with and in the course of the discussions she learned a lot about what was going on elsewhere in the school. For example, her target of working on the library website was removed from the plan because the line manager advised that the school was concentrating on setting up a VLE. Instead, a target relating to library involvement in talks and training about the VLE was introduced.

Frances also wanted to develop a 'whole-school' approach to information literacy but through talking about what was realistic and timely they arrived at some objectives that were challenging, yet attainable. At least, the line manager saw no problem with three science teachers allowing Frances to run her pilot project in their lessons. Frances, on her own, would never have committed herself to something this specific in case others would think she was being presumptuous. What is more, she knew that rolling her ideas out to more classes in subsequent years would feature in their discussions as part of the next planning cycle.

Evidence

Successfully implementing new ideas and new technologies or designs is an important part of what we do, but it is vital that the benefit and value they add for students can be measured. It is not enough to advocate new initiatives without supporting evidence.

Most teachers have to provide statistical analysis from their lessons to show progression in their students' work. They can then use this information to change the lesson plans if it shows that the students are not achieving targets or are finding some aspects of work less easy to understand than others. Using the evidence-based 'action research' approach can also help a librarian to introduce innovative ideas.

A review of the literature shows that innovation is recognized and celebrated with a number of different awards by school library organizations and other libraries worldwide. These include the International Association of School Librarianship, the School Library Association of Victoria, the California School Library Association and the University of Wollongong, New South Wales. Their websites are listed at 'Websites cited' on page 166. Their awards focus on innovations that are an integral part of teaching and learning in the school and where success can be measured in terms of outcome.

The criteria for innovative practice includes:

- a collaboration or partnership beyond the school library
- new programmes for or approaches to wider reading, curriculum development or curriculum support for learning areas or school curriculum initiatives
- innovation as a catalyst for change
- adding new value for library stakeholders
- identifying and applying solutions rather than presenting problems
- fostering an environment or culture that supports risk-taking and the opportunity to learn from mistakes
- challenging what is done and the way it is done.

School Library Association guidelines on developing learning resource centre web pages also emphasize the importance of being innovative and keeping up with current trends: 'The 21st century LRC needs to be at the forefront of curriculum innovation and ICT development if it is to act as the school's natural information centre and place of reference' (Murphy, 2003).

Of course, it is not only school library organizations that recognize the importance of innovation. The Headmasters' and Headmistresses' Conference (HMC) in the UK has published a series of case studies of innovation and good practice in HMC schools. These include an example of a school library project on teaching information literacy skills and a case study of a school where the library acts as 'an information hub for the whole college community' and 'librarians manage the school website, intranet and extranet, coordinating the organisation of content from the whole community' (Trafford, 2006).

Managing change

When planning to innovate there are a number of things to consider.

The scope of the innovation

Ask yourself these questions:

- How big is the change that you are trying to introduce?
- What range of activities is needed in order to make it successful?
- Who needs to be involved?

Clarity about these elements is vital.

The nature of your organization

It is important to understand how the school works and how ready it is to engage with change. This will help to ensure that the processes used and steps taken fit comfortably with the way the school operates. If we manage change in a way that is not congruent with the environment it will at best produce more conflict than necessary and at worst not produce the results that we want. Innovation involves many different activities, and the paths to achieving the same result will look different in different schools.

Key factors in implementing a change

It is important to do a systematic analysis of the factors in school that will support the innovation and those that might hinder it. This enables us to draw up a sensible action plan based on our real environments (see Appendix 8 for a useful tool to map key factors).

Prioritizing activities

Managing any change involves us in choosing priorities. What should we work on in order to support the process of change as effectively as possible? None of us have unlimited time, energy or resources, so we need to focus activity on what we think will be most productive in our environment. What do we really need to pay attention to as a matter of priority? When everything appears to be important people can be reluctant to prioritize. However, studies of change have shown that success is more likely when a clear focus is sustained on a limited number of factors.

Working with people

This is probably the most challenging part of managing change. We need to think hard about what we want people to do differently, how to present it to them and how to support them in changing. We also need to be clear about the effect that the innovation will have on our own roles and activities.

Process and principles of managing change

The People's Network Change Management Toolkit (Information Management Associates, 2004) reminds us that 'significant innovation will take time' and that most significant change processes are likely to take at least three years. The toolkit outlines the process of change and the different activities needed at each stage. See Appendix 9 for an outline of these steps, which are based on the work of Michael Fullan (2007).

This toolkit also spells out some important principles about monitoring the progress of the innovation, finding supporters and allies, having a clear vision, choosing something that will have early impact, communicating progress and success to other people, and realizing that not everyone will be prepared to change. All these principles must be taken into consideration if the change or innovation is to be successful (Appendix 8).

Using whole-school processes and the key change agents

In Chapter 5 we said that it is important to offer solutions to senior management rather than airing our complaints or problems. The same holds true when we attempt to innovate or manage change. The following vignette shows how, by presenting a positive initiative, change can be successfully introduced.

Few pupils at Linda's school borrowed reading books from their school library; as librarian, Linda was due to meet her line manager to discuss this. She had read that the subject of supporting 'gifted and talented' students was becoming a high priority in many schools, often with extra money attached. She knew that this would be a golden opportunity to show what she could do. Using the UK school librarians' self-evaluation document (Markless and Streatfield, 2004), she prepared a list of possible action points, which she then included in a memo to the senior teacher in charge of the initiative. Her colleague welcomed her unsolicited contribution as supportive and positive and followed up every one of the ideas. Linda was invited to be part of the working group to take things forward and her line manager was impressed that rather than complaining about lack of use Linda had strong proposals to bring about change.

By linking her ideas to a whole-school initiative and submitting these to a senior teacher, Linda has successfully matched her action points to a perceived need in the school and found a supporter and advocate for her cause. These are two of the essential steps identified by Michael Fullan (2007) in the first phase of implementing change. However, the following assumptions must also be made:

- that conflict and disagreement are not only inevitable but fundamental
- that no amount of knowledge will make it totally clear what action should be taken
- that change is a frustrating, discouraging business so expect and plan for setbacks. Don't be discouraged when they happen; it would be more surprising if they didn't (Information Management Associates, 2004).

The following vignette shows that even when we are confident in our role and feel reasonably safe in proposing a new initiative, we can be discouraged and encounter setbacks.

Barbara had established herself as a respected member of staff at her state secondary school so when she offered to attend Year 7 and 8 parent/teacher consultation evenings to give advice to parents on how to support their children's reading, the English teachers were very keen on the idea (even if some were a little puzzled that she should have 'volunteered' for extra evening work). Librarians from other schools who heard about the innovation were very impressed and one even went on to establish herself in a similar role. However, even though Barbara could hear her teaching colleagues recommending that parents speak to her, Year 7 parents seemed to be too nervous, overwhelmed by the situation and fixed on seeing every teacher to spare the time. Year 8 parents were more open to the suggestion, with 19 of them seeking consultations during the three-hour period, but many others ignored the teachers' prompting. The limited take-up was very disappointing because Barbara had felt that the idea was a huge leap forward.

Barbara will need to consider whether in future years her presence will become more accepted and maybe even expected, or whether she could spend the time more usefully on other things, because 'Effective change or innovation takes time' (Hargreaves and Hopkins, 1994). Meanwhile, she was fortunate that her spirits were sustained by the fact that the English teachers had so readily taken up her idea, demonstrating their trust and respect.

Innovation inevitably involves change, which by its nature can be problematic and may meet resistance from other members of our school community. Managing change successfully can be achieved if we understand the various processes involved.

Innovation is difficult and uncomfortable and requires courage and determination. However, it can be exciting and reaffirms why we continue to be school librarians. It is challenging but necessary to maintain inspiration and integration. Being innovative is at the heart of thinking and acting strategically.

We wrote this book with the aim of prompting school librarians to stand back from their day-to-day activity and critically re-examine their values, philosophy and what defines their professional practice. Innovation is the best place to end this book because it is through innovation that we renew our professional identity.

References

American Association of School Librarians (2007) *Standards for the 21st Century Learner*, Chicago, IL, AASL, www.ala.org/ala/aasl/aaslproftools/learningstandards/ AASL_Learning_Standards_2007.pdf.

Barrett, L. and Douglas, J. (2004) *CILIP Guidelines for Secondary School Libraries*, London, Facet Publishing.

Bennett, S. (2003) *Libraries Designed for Learning*, Washington, DC, Council on Library and Information Resources.

Bloom, B. S. (ed.) (1956) *Taxonomy of Educational Objectives: the classification of educational goals. Handbook I: the cognitive domain*, New York, David McKay.

Brabazon, T. (2008) We Can't Let Schools Become Book-free Zones, *Times Higher Education Supplement*, 31 May, www.timeshighereducation.co.uk/story.asp?sectioncode =26&storycode=402219&c=1.

Bradnock, M. (2007) *Blogs and Bytes: ICT and the secondary school library*, Swindon, School Library Association.

Brighouse, T. (2008) *What Makes a Good School Now?*, London, Network Continuum.

Chartered Institute of Library and Information Professionals (2008) *Framework of Qualifications*, www.cilip.org.uk/qualificationschartership/ FrameworkofQualifications.

Christie, J. (2008) Stand Up for the Brand 'Libraries = Books = Reading', *CILIP Update*, **7** (5), May, 26.

Clyde, L. A. (2004) Homosexuality in Literature for Young People: the story and access to the story. In Moore, P. et al. (eds), *IASL Reports, 2004: from Aesop to e-book, the story goes on*, Erie, PA, International Association of School Librarianship.

Cohen, L., Manion, L. and Morrison, K. (2007) *Research Methods in Education*, 6th edn, London, Routledge.

Conroy, H. (2006) *Information Skills for Teachers: a report for the Eduserv Foundation Information Literacy Programme*, www.netskills.ac.uk/content/projects/eduserv-info-lit/ NetskillsEduservInfoSkills.pdf.

Costa, A. L. and Karrick, B. (2000) *Habits of Mind: a developmental series*, 4 vols, Alexandria, VA, Association for Supervision and Curriculum Development.

Department for Children, Schools and Families (2008a) Knight: extended projects will help prepare students for work and university, 14 August, Press Notice 2008/0173, London, DCSF, www.dcsf.gov.uk/pns/DisplayPN.cgi?pn_id=2008_0173.

Department for Children, Schools and Families (2006) *Leading in Learning: developing thinking skills at Key Stage 3*, Standards Site,

www.standards.dfes.gov.uk/secondary/keystage3/all/respub/
ws_lil_ts.

Department for Education and Employment (2000) *Key Stage 3 National Strategy: literacy across the curriculum,* London, DfEE.

Department for Education and Employment (2001) *Key Stage 3 National Strategy: numeracy across the curriculum*, London, DfEE.

Department for Education and Skills (2004) *Pedagogy and Practice: teaching and learning in secondary schools*, London, DfES. DCSF ref. no. 0423 2004, resources pack to complement the Key Stage 3 National Strategy Training.

Encarta (2009) Definition of 'inspiration', http://encarta.msn.com/thesaurus_561577636/ inspiration.html.

Festinger, L. (1957) *A Theory of Cognitive Dissonance*, Stanford, CA, Stanford University Press.

Fielding, M. and Bragg, S. (2003) *Students as Researchers: making a difference*, Cambridge, Pearson Publishing.

Fish, D. and De Cossart, L. (2006) Thinking Outside The (Tick) Box: rescuing professionalism and professional judgement, *Medical Education*, **40** (5), 403–4.

Forsyth, D. R. (2006) *Group Dynamics*, 4th edn, Belmont, CA, Thomson Wadsworth.

Foucault, M. (1972) *The Archaeology of Knowledge*, London, Tavistock Publications.

Fullan, M. G. (2007)*The New Meaning of Educational Change*, 4th edn, London, Routledge.

Gorard, S. (2001) *Quantitative Methods in Educational Research: the role of numbers made easy*, New York, Continuum International.

Habermas, J. (1987) *The Philosophical Discourse of Modernity*, Cambridge, Polity Press.

Hallam, S. and Price, J. (1998) Can the Use of Background Music Improve the Behaviour and Academic Performance of Children with Emotional and Behavioural Difficulties?, *British Journal of Special Education*, **25** (2), June, www.behaviour4learning.ac.uk/attachments/ 51c2b0e9-7c0c-4650-b884-e8f89b6c253f.pdf.

Hargreaves, A. (1994; 2000) *Changing Teachers, Changing Times: teachers' work and culture in the postmodern age*, London, Cassell (1994); London and New York, Continuum International.

Hargreaves, A. (2000) *Changing Teachers, Changing Times*.

Hargreaves, D. H. and Hopkins, D. (1994) *Development Planning for School Improvement*, London, Cassell.

Hargreaves, D. H. and Hopkins, D. (2005) *The Empowered School: management and practice of development*, London and New York, Continuum International.

Improvement and Development Agency (2005) *Library Services Peer Review Benchmark*, London, I&DEA, www.idea.gov.uk/idk/aio/1155040.

Information Management Associates (2004) *People's Network Change Management Toolkit*, London, Museums, Libraries and Archives Council, http://mlac.gov.uk/programmes/peoples_network/ peoples_network_archive/change.

International Federation of Library Associations (2006) *IFLA/UNESCO School Libraries Manifesto: the school library in teaching and learning for all*, The Hague, Netherlands, www.ifla.org/VII/s11/pubs/manifest.htm.

Kuhlthau, C. C. (1993) *Seeking Meaning: a process approach to library and information services*, Norwood, NJ, Ablex Publishing.

Lance, K. C., Rodney, M. J. and Hamilton-Pennell, C. (2000) *How School Librarians Help Kids Achieve Standards: the Second Colorado Study*, Colorado, Library Research Service Colorado State Library. www.lrs.org/documents/lmcstudies/CO/execsumm.pdf.

Lankes, D. (2009) We Live in Shakespearean Times. In *The Participatory Librarian Starter Kit*, http://ptbed.org/blog/?p=692.

Lennon, J. (2007) Loreto College Whole School Reading Project, *Hertfordshire Schools Library Service Newsletter* (Summer).

Lyotard, J. (1979) *The Postmodern Condition: a report on knowledge*, Manchester, Manchester University Press.

McCall, M. W. Jr. (2004) Taking the Lead on Innovation; Available from http://discussionleader.hbsp.com/hmu/2008/02/taking-the-lead-on-innovation-1.php.

McMenemy, D. (2007) Invasion of the Body Snatchers, *CILIP Update*, **6** (4), April, 18–19.

Markless, S. and Streatfield, D. R. (2004) *Improve Your Library: a self-evaluation process for secondary school libraries and learning resource centres*, 2 vols, London, DfES, www.teachernet.gov.uk/docbank/index.cfm?id=6616.

Marland, M. (ed.) (1981) *Information Skills in the Secondary Curriculum: recommendations of a Working Group sponsored by the British Library and the Schools Council*, London, Methuen Educational.

Maslow, A. H. (1998) *Towards a Psychology of Being*, 3rd edn, London, Wiley.

Mind Tools (2008) *Force Field Analysis: understanding the pressures for and against change*, www.mindtools.com/pages/article/newTED_06.htm.

Murphy, R. (2003) *Going Online: developing LRC web pages*, SLA Guidelines, Swindon, School Library Association.

National Literacy Trust (2007) *Reading Connects: building whole school reading communities*, www.literacytrust.org.uk/readingconnects/competition.html.

Newton, C. and Tarrant, T. (1992) *Managing Change in Schools*, London, Routledge.

Ofsted (2006) *Good School Libraries: making a difference to learning*, London, Ofsted.

Oncken, W. Jr and Wass, D. L. (1999) Management Time: who's got the monkey?, *Harvard Business Review*, Nov–Dec, 1–8, www.vlgma.org/vertical/Sites/%7BA8553521-0E8F-4DB8-A0F2-FA053AC29FF7%7D/uploads/%7BF56F0272-7358-4D74-B0A6-672D6D950AAE%7D.PDF.

Pedley, D. (2001) email to eLRARG mailing list.

Qualifications and Curriculum Authority (2007) *A Framework of Personal, Learning and Thinking Skills*, London, QCA, www.qca.org.uk/libraryAssets/media/PLTS_framework.pdf.

Quinn, T. (2003) The Teacher Talent Trove, *Kappa Delta Pi Record*, Fall, 26–9, http://eric.ed.gov/ERICDocs/data/ericdocs2sql/content_storage_01/0000019b/80/3d/12/45.pdf.

Rayner, S. and Gunter, H. (2005) Rethinking Leadership:

perspectives on remodelling practice, *Educational Review*, **57** (2), 151–61.

Reynolds, G. (2008) *Presentation Zen: inspiration matters*, www.presentationzen.com/presentationzen/2008/02/if-your-present.html%20.

Roberts, N. (1992) New Model Librarians: a question of philosophy? A review article, *Journal of Librarianship and Information Science*, **24**, September, 169–73.

Roberts, S. and Rowley, J. (2008) *Leadership: the challenge for the information profession*, London, Facet Publishing.

Rogers, J. and Frost, B. (2006) *Every Child Matters: empowering the student voice*, London, DfES.

[Scholastic] Research Foundation (2008) *School libraries work!*, research foundation paper, 3rd edn, Danbury, CT, Scholastic Library Publishing, www.scholastic.com/grolierdocs/home.html.

Schon, D. (1983) *The Reflective Practitioner: how professionals think in action*, London, Temple Smith.

School Librarians' Network – Yahoo egroup. Founded in 1998. Now has over 800 members, http://groups.yahoo.com/group/sln/.

Small, R. V. et al. (2007) *New York State's School Libraries and Media Specialists: an impact study*, Syracuse, NY, Center for Digital Literacy, Syracuse University, www.nyla.org/content/user_1/Preliminary_Report_Small.pdf.

Starrs, J. (2002) *School Libraries in Northern Ireland: an investigation into their current and potential contribution to learning: a report on research conducted for the Association of Chief*

Librarians, Northern Ireland,
www.belb.org.uk/libraries/full_report.pdf.

Stenhouse, L. (1975) *An Introduction to Curriculum Research and Development*, London, Heinemann.

Streatfield, D. R. and Markless, S. (1994) *Invisible Learning? The contribution of school libraries to teaching and learning*, Library and Information Research Report 98, London, British Library Research and Development Department.

Stronach, I. et al. (2002) Towards an Uncertain Politics of Professionalism: teacher and nurse identities in flux, *Journal of Education Policy*, **17** (1), 109–38.

Swaffield, S. (ed.) (2008) *Unlocking Assessment: understanding for reflection and application*, London, Routledge.

Taylor, L. and Guiney, P. (2008) Leading the Way to Excellence. *Library and Information Gazette*, 25 July–7 August, 27.

Todd, R. J. (2001) Transitions for Preferred Futures of School Libraries: knowledge space, not information place; connections, not collections; actions, not positions; evidence not advocacy, keynote address, *IASL Conference*, New Zealand,
www.iasl-slo.org/virtualpaper2001.html.

Todd, R. J.(2005) Information Literacy and Enquiry Learning: the role of the library, keynote lecture, *School Library Association Conference*, Surrey University, Guildford.

Todd, R. J. (2005b) School Libraries, Productive Pedagogy and the Leading of Learning, presentation at *School Library Association of Victoria* Conference,

www.slav.schools.net.au/downloads/08pastpapers/15learners/
RToddAug2005.ppt.

Trafford, B. (ed.) (2006) *i² = independent + innovative: examples
of innovation in HMC schools*, London, John Catt Educational
Ltd.

Tripp, D. (1993) *Critical Incidents in Teaching: developing
professional judgement*, London, Routledge.

University of Wollongong (2003) *UOW Library Management
Handbook Section D11: Innovation Management Policy*,
Wollongong, Australia: University of Wollongong, NSW,
www.library.uow.edu.au/content/groups/public/@web/@lib/
documents/doc/uow026921.pdf.

Webb, C. (2009) *Can Librarians and Teachers Work Together?*,
Canterbury, Canterbury Christchurch University,
Unpublished doctorate.

Wenger, E. (1998) *Communities of Practice: learning, meaning and
identity*, Cambridge, Cambridge University Press.

Williams, D. A. and Coles, L. (2003) *The Use of Research by
Teachers: information literacy, access and attitudes*, Aberdeen,
Robert Gordon University,
www.rgu.ac.uk/files/ACF8497.pdf.

Williams, D. A., Coles, L. and Wavell, C. (2002) *Impact of
School Library Services on Achievement and Learning in Primary
Schools*, Aberdeen, School of Information and Media,
Faculty of Management, The Robert Gordon University,
www.rgu.ac.uk/files/ACF1C8D.pdf.

Williams, D. A. and Wavell, C. (2006) *Information Literacy in the
Classroom: secondary school teachers' conceptions*, Research Report
15, Aberdeen, Department of Information Management,

Aberdeen Business School, The Robert Gordon University.

Williams, D. A. and Wavell, C (2007) Making Connections: the nature and impact of information mediation in the development of information literacy in schools, paper presented at *Information: Interactions and Impact Conference,* The Robert Gordon University, Aberdeen.

Wilson, P. (1983) *Second-hand Knowledge: an inquiry into cognitive authority,* Santa Barbara, CA, Greenwood Press.

Websites cited

California School Library Association (2007) The Innovation Award,
www.schoolibrary.org/awa/pdf/Innovation_Award_08.pdf.

International Association of School Libraries (2008) School Library Technology Innovation Award,
www.iasl-online.org/awards/technology-award.htm.

School Library Association (2007) School Librarian of the Year Award,
www.sla.org.uk/slya-2007.php.

School Library Association of Victoria (2008) The SLAV Innovator's Grant,
www.slav.schools.net.au/awards.html#innovator.

Appendix 1
Levels of education

Level		Descriptor
1	Organizer	No instruction: • self-service search in an organized collection
2	Lecturer	Orienteering instruction: • single session • overview of services, policies and location of facility and collection • no specific problem.
3	Instructor	Single-source instruction: • variety of independent sessions • instruction on one type of source to address specific problems.
4	Tutor	Strategy instruction: • series of sessions • instruction on sequence of sources to address specific problem.
5	Counsellor	Process instruction • holistic interaction over time • instruction on identifying and interpreting information to address evolving problem.

Source: Kuhlthau, 1993

Appendix 2
School library self-evaluation questions

Library self-evaluation	Secondary school self-evaluation form	Evidence examples
Key question 1 How high are standards?	3a How well do learners achieve, and how high are their standards?	Assessment of learning of students in library-based work Examples of work produced
Key question 2 How well are pupils' attitudes, values and personal qualities developed?	4 How good is the overall personal development and well-being of the learners?	Evidence of consultation with students Range of supportive materials Overall atmosphere in the library
Key question 3 How effective are teaching and learning?	5a How good is the quality of teaching and learning?	External viewpoints – local authority audits, Ofsted, HM Inspectorate Visiting librarians (can help to establish the library as a good model in eyes of external and therefore of internal eyes) Assessment of learning of students in library-based work
Key question 4 How well does library provision meet pupils' needs?	5. The quality of provision 5b How well do the curriculum and other activities meet the range of needs and interests of learners?	Feedback from students, parents and teachers Record of resources used in research work
Key question 5 How well are pupils guided and supported?	5c How well are learners guided and supported?	Assessment data on student reading and writing Homework Club reports to tutors to highlight regular and hardworking attenders Library displays

Library self-evaluation	Secondary school self-evaluation form	Evidence examples
Key question 6 How effectively does the library work with parents and the community?	2 What are the views of learners, parents/carers and other stakeholders, including hard to reach groups, and how do you know?	Letters to home about Homework Club and reading achievements Library newsletter
Key question 7 How well is the LRC/library led and managed?	6a What is the overall effectiveness of leadership and management?	INSET – presentation to staff Library publications for staff and students Feedback to staff and governors Annual report Participation in school events, staff meetings and working parties Range of activities planned and delivered

Markless and Streatfield (2004)

Appendix 3
Sample survey of teachers' perceptions of the role of the school librarian

I am collaborating on writing a book on the strategic management of school libraries. As part of this I am looking at the perceptions of other people within the school of what a school librarian is and does.

I should be very grateful if you could help me with an idea of how you perceive me and what I do, and what your expectations are. If you have any comments about perceptions of librarians in previous schools, that would be great too.

Even a few words would be useful.

You do not need to identify yourself, but it would be very useful if you could indicate whether you are a head of department, or in charge of a subject, how long you have been teaching and how long you have been in the school. Just return this page to my pigeonhole.

How long in school?
❑ new this year   ❑ 1–3 years   ❑ over 3 years

Teacher Yes / No

If yes: HoD or in charge of a subject   Yes / No

How long teaching?
❑ NQT–2 years   ❑ 3–10 years   ❑ 11 years or longer

Appendix 4
SWOT analysis

Focus: for example developing a new approach to assessing IL, introducing a new reading activity.

Strengths, e.g. advantages; knowledge; capabilities; resources; experience; likely benefits; value; cultural, behavioural and attitudinal aspects?	Weaknesses, e.g. disadvantages, gaps in capabilities or knowledge; timescale; workload pressures; effect on core activities; resources; reliability of plan; predictability of outcome; level of support?
Opportunities, e.g. organizational trends; educational agenda; new partnerships; technology development; seasonal, fashion or cultural influences?	Threats, e.g. political effects; destabilization of core activities, sustainable finance; loss of key partners; IT developments; competing services or activities?

An example of a SWOT analysis

Meena worked as a librarian at a large comprehensive school. Generally the library was well used but she had noticed some departments seldom made use of the facilities, especially those for maths. She was aware that some other school librarians in her area had already been successful in encouraging classes into libraries to do number puzzles. Meena did not feel confident that she had the expertise to go to the department directly and chose to do a SWOT analysis on whether she should explore this idea further.

Strengths	Weaknesses
• Other schools have used this successfully • Library well stocked with puzzle books • Number puzzles popular generally	• I'm not very good at number puzzles myself and may not be much help during the class
Opportunities	**Threats**
• Will look good at next inspection that Maths department is using the library • Will help students' numerical abilities • Will meet demands of the Library Development Plan • Will help pupils become comfortable with the library environment in a different subject • Could lead to more projects	• Maths department may say they are too busy with curriculum • Other departments may compete for library time and may get upset if Maths dept books but don't turn up

Meena decided she had enough Strengths and Opportunities information to make a strong case to the Maths department for an experimental lesson. This proved successful and has now become an established part of the scheme of work for younger students. On the back of this Meena has also established a puzzle club at lunchtimes assisted by older students (who can help solve the problems!).

Appendix 5
Choosing priorities in development planning – sample grid

One source (Hargreaves and Hopkins, 1994) suggests we create a grid and list down one side all our proposed activities that would contribute towards the school targets. Across the top of the grid place these measures: unavoidable, urgent, desirable, large size and scope, small size and scope, strong roots (already part of the school's established practice), weak roots, strong links to priorities and weak links to priorities.

Activity	Unavoidable	Urgent	Desirable	Large size + scope	Small size + scope	Strong roots	Weak roots	Strong links to priorities	Weak links to priorities
Year 9 reading challenge	✓			✓		✓		✓	
Guitar-building workshop			✓		✓		✓	✓	
Poetry jam sessions at lunchtime			✓		✓		✓	✓	
Introduce extra reading assessment in autumn term for Year 7	✓	✓	✓	✓		✓		✓	
Library asst training			✓		✓	✓		✓	

Appendix 6
An example of a completed self-evaluation

Summary Sheet *Key question 3: How effective are teaching and learning?*

Strand 3b: Co-operation between LRC staff and teaching staff to ensure effective learning

Reason for choice of key question and strand:

We work very well with some curriculum areas but there are a number of departments that use the library as a room without drawing on the librarian's support and expertise in any way.

Indicator	Level awarded in last evaluation	Evidence collected	Level awarded (1–5)	What should the LRC do to improve?
i. Do LRC staff and teachers plan and teach collaboratively for LRC-based lessons and courses?	N/a	Diary showing lessons taught collaboratively; worksheets	3	Work on formalizing collaborative teaching by preparing formal lesson plans for lessons
ii. Do LRC and teaching staff collaborate to ensure that research and study skills are taught and assessed in appropriate places throughout the curriculum?	N/a	Record of recent work as research mentor for individual A-level students in History and Media Studies; Lesson taught to A level Geography & A level Science; Discussions with Science teachers about 'Science in the News' project. Induction programme for Year 7	2	Map Information Literacy Skills delivery in the library across the years and use the process to raise discussion with teachers. (References in Schemes of Work would be a more long-term whole-school issue)

Indicator	Level awarded in last evaluation	Evidence collected	Level awarded (1–5)	What should the LRC do to improve?
iii. Do departments include effective LRC use in their schemes of work and homework tasks?	N/a	Annual reports to individual subject departments	4	Analyse homework tasks for indications of LRC use
iv. Do LRC staff work in partnership with the SENCO, Gifted and Talented co-ordinator and EAL co-ordinator?	N/a	Reports to SENCO and G&T co-ordinator	3	
v. Are teachers involved in the selection of LRC resources and in the development of the LRC and its role within the school?	N/a	Examples of teachers' written requests for stock and minutes of meetings with individual heads of dept.		Step up reporting to departments so that it becomes an annual review
vi. Is there an effective induction programme to the LRC for all staff new to the school?	N/a	Librarian takes part in the induction programme for new staff – 15 minute talk. Outline of Library use in Staff Handbook	3	Interview last year's new teachers using 'Questions for Staff' document
vii. Do LRC staff lead INSET and provide informal training for teaching staff?	N/a	Examples of ad hoc training and informal discussions (No formal INSET)	3	

Support required to enable the LRC to improve: Overall level reached: 3
Advice from line manager on lesson planning

Appendix 7
Some possibilities for gaining inspiration in the UK

1 Professional groups such as School Libraries Group, Youth Libraries Group, School Library Association

These may be of varying importance depending on the location of our schools because levels of activity vary in different regions, but they can play an important part in keeping us up to date, networked with our colleagues and excited about our jobs.

2 Formal courses – from one-day workshops to Master's programmes

Meg attended a course about promoting reading where a number of librarians gave book talks. The variety of approaches stimulated her to become creative in her presentations to students, who responded by borrowing and reading more.

A group of school librarians studied for a Master's in Education. They found it deepened their understanding of their educational context and gave them insights into learning and curriculum development. They continued to meet after the course ended, exchanging ideas and gaining the impetus to challenge and change their practice.

3 Conferences run by professional bodies

International Association of School Librarians
www.iasl-online.org/
Librarian's Information Literacy Conference (LILAC)
www.lilacconference.com/
School Libraries Group (a special interest group of CILIP)
www.cilip.org.uk/specialinterestgroups/bysubject/school
School Library Association
www.sla.org.uk/
Specialist Schools Trust
www.specialistschools.org.uk/

4 Local self-help groups

School librarians in one local authority decided to start a folder to share ideas and resources developed in their individual schools. This has proved invaluable in recording and disseminating good practice.

5 Online communities

The internet has opened up the possibility of communicating with many librarians and others elsewhere. There are lists specifically for school librarians, abroad and in the UK, as well as lists dealing with topics of particular interest to us, such as children's literature. The School Library Network can be particularly inspiring because of the sheer volume of ideas posted on it. Even though some ideas may be inappropriate to our circumstances, the number available and the fact that we can get help in working out the details make it more likely that we will be inspired.

Hermione read on the Child-Lit email list that *Holes* by Louis Sachar was proving a great hit with reluctant readers, particularly boys, in America. As a result she was able to persuade a number of the boys in her school that reading could be fun, and eventually the book was adopted by the English department as a reader for Year 8 students.

Ron wanted to increase use of the library by reluctant readers and found a suggestion on the School Library Network list that graphic novels could help. By asking for suggestions he was able to compile a list of appropriate titles, which he promoted through displays and a poster campaign throughout the school.

---

6 Exhibitions

Exhibitions such as BETT, the Education Show and the Library & Information Show enable us to explore new resources and initiatives, which may be appropriate to our schools. There may also be seminars from government agencies and educational gurus which can inspire us to explore how we can make them relevant to our library service.

7 Journals, newspapers, books and websites

There is much material published in print or on the internet which is relevant to school libraries.

- You may start with a generic professional journal, e.g. *Update*, which presents articles from practitioners across the whole field of librarianship.
- The more focused journals such as *School Libraries in View*, from CILIP's School Libraries Group, and the *School*

Librarian, the journal of the School Library Association, are particularly good at providing fodder to inspire those in the early years of their job as a school librarian. Their direct relevance provides support.

- The international school library journals, especially those from America and Australia, can jolt us out of our comfort zones and make us re-examine our assumptions about what might be possible. Some of them are totally research-based, which can add an extra dimension to our deliberations. Research on information literacy or what a school librarian needs to put in place to make a real difference can inspire deep reflection and review of practice.

- We may also look at academic journals dealing with children's literature and learning, or at subject-related journals, which may help us select relevant stock.

As we mentioned earlier in Chapter 6, it is important to draw on as wide a range of material as possible when searching for inspiration. A wide variety of ideas can inspire us to change.

Appendix 8
Tools for managing change

Example of a force field analysis

Forces for change   **Forces against change**

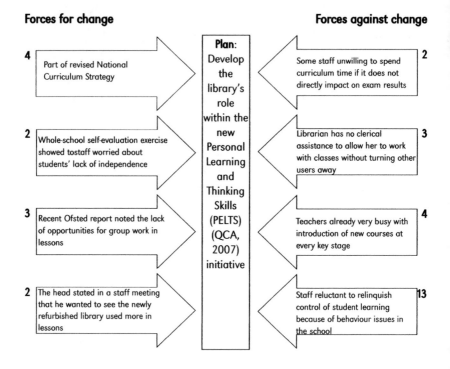

4 Part of revised National Curriculum Strategy

2 Some staff unwilling to spend curriculum time if it does not directly impact on exam results

2 Whole-school self-evaluation exercise showed tostaff worried about students' lack of independence

3 Librarian has no clerical assistance to allow her to work with classes without turning other users away

3 Recent Ofsted report noted the lack of opportunities for group work in lessons

4 Teachers already very busy with introduction of new courses at every key stage

2 The head stated in a staff meeting that he wanted to see the newly refurbished library used more in lessons

13 Staff reluctant to relinquish control of student learning because of behaviour issues in the school

Plan: Develop the library's role within the new Personal Learning and Thinking Skills (PELTS) (QCA, 2007) initiative

Appendix 9
Managing change: process and principles

The change process: phases of implementation

The process outlined below indicates what librarians need to pay attention to when trying to innovate. It is not a blueprint or programme for managing change as the elements will look different in different locations. The steps below are based on the work of Michael Fullan (Fullan, 2007).

Stage 1: Initiation
Tie into perceived needs and priorities:

- Find a strong advocate to go out and talk to those likely to be affected and to get concrete support from influential people in the school.
- Consult widely. At this stage it is not usually a good idea to try to involve everyone. However, those likely to be affected need to be kept informed of what is happening, what is being considered, etc.
- Develop clear processes to engage people with the change and to make developments as transparent as possible (e.g. checklists, exercises for students). Everyone needs a good idea of what they should be doing differently.

At this stage the focus is on the innovation: what is it all about? What are the implications? How important and relevant is it?

Stage 2: Implementation

- All change needs a co-ordinator to keep things moving and to orchestrate the process. Co-ordinators need to be sensitive and flexible.
- Local empowerment must be supported. This means enabling other staff to take some control over the process. Perhaps they can be involved in deciding priorities or what to do first. Some local adaptation should be encouraged. Teachers will always want to adapt an innovation to their own teaching approach.
- Be ready with advice, technical assistance and trouble-shooting, vital components of any implementation. Too often such support is readily available near the beginning of any innovation but fizzles out when people really need help.
- Tangible benefits and rewards of the innovation need to be made apparent (early concrete practices). Show what the innovation can do to meet a perceived need in the school. Are more students engaging with a subject? Are more boys reading? Publicize examples of success. People are more likely to be persuaded by seeing the benefits than by being told how good an innovation is or will be.

At this stage the main focus is on people: helping and encouraging colleagues to adopt the innovation.

Stage 3: Incorporation

- Make sure that the innovation has been built into institutional mechanisms and systems, and the way in which the institution functions (e.g. staff development; budgeting, curriculum development and assessment), or the committee structure may need to be changed.
- Competing demands from new initiatives, policies and government requirements may cause attention and resources to be switched away from what we are trying to achieve. How can the time, energy and resources needed to continue this work be protected in the face of competing demands? Does something else need to be thrown out or demoted to prevent too many conflicting demands being made on staff? Who is in a position to sort out these priorities?
- Induction for new staff at all levels must incorporate the innovation.
- Build up a critical mass of users. This will help keep up momentum and show how important it is to sustain the change. However, do not expect everyone to adopt an innovation.

At this stage the main focus is on the organization and how it functions. Can it adapt its systems and procedures to accommodate the new demands? Or will it merely try to bolt this innovation on to an existing bureaucracy, which means that the change is unlikely to stick in the long term?

Those trying to innovate need to understand how the change process occurs but they also need to keep some general principles in mind. These are helpful when things are not proceeding as hoped or when we get impatient at the often slow rate of progress.

Adapted from: Information Management Associates, 2004

Managing change –some key principles

- **Monitor the progress** of the innovation carefully. Be prepared to step in and slow things down or change direction if the innovating is moving too quickly or is not having the desired impact (not a good return on the investment of time and effort).
- **Build alliances:** network to find supporters and advocates. We cannot do it by ourselves.
- **Think big**: we all need a clear vision of what success looks like and are sustained by what we might achieve – the overall aims of the innovation. But act small: plan for steady progress and take measured steps towards the vision.
- **Avoid 'brute sanity'**: It is tempting when trying to promote change to give lots of clear, loud messages to staff about how wonderful the innovation is, how it will revolutionize student learning/reading/motivation etc. This is brute sanity. And if the messages are said often enough and loud enough, staff will tend to back off and build barriers to hide behind! Missionaries tend to make poor change agents. People need space to work out their position and decide how to deal with the innovation.
- **Get some early concrete practices in place:** Choose something that will have some impact fairly quickly but don't

worry if it is not perfect. An early showcase of what is possible will help persuade and build alliances.

- **Keep people informed** about progress, successes, impact; publicize your services; show benefits in practice.
- **Be prepared to work very hard**.
- **Do not expect all or even most to change:** One useful reminder of what to expect is the adage that 30% of people will be prepared to support and participate in change (if it is worthwhile); 40% will keep their distance and will need to be persuaded with good evidence that the innovation meets a real need and is worth the investment of their time and energy – they can be won over; 30% will not change.

Use these principles as a package. You cannot just choose the ones that you like if you want change to be effective.

Adapted from: Information Management Associates, 2004

Index

academic status
line-management systems 93
professionalism 93
ACAS *see* Advice, Conciliation
    and Arbitration Service
action, innovation 146–9
Advice, Conciliation and
    Arbitration Service
    (ACAS), dichotomy 56–7
assessment for learning,
    inspiration 117–18
assumptions, questioning,
    inspiration 116–17
audit trail, professionalism   81
awards
    innovation 150–1
    inspiration 109–10
awareness, dichotomy 54, 55

awareness-raising, information
    literacy 37

balance, professionalism 92
balkanized culture, school
    culture 67
behaviourist approach
    learning 72
    teaching approach 69–70
beliefs re-examination,
    dichotomy 57–8
benchmarking
data sharing 84–5
    peer reviews 84–5
    professionalism 83–6
    standards 85–6
    UNESCO/IFLA School
    Libraries' Manifesto 85–6

Booked Up scheme,
integration 141
books, inspiration 178-9

change *see also* managing
change
implementing 152
innovation 151–6
inspiration 105, 107
Chartered Institute for Library
and Information
Professionals (CILIP)
Chartership Framework
11
professionalism 2
Chartered Institute of Personnel and Development
(CIPD), dichotomy 57
chartered librarians 1–2
CILIP *see* Chartered Institute
for Library and
Information Professionals
CIPD *see* Chartered Institute
of Personnel and
Development
classes of students, service
considerations 65
clerical support,
professionalism 82–3

cognitive authority,
professional identity 23
cognitive/constructivist
approach, learning 72
cognitive dissonance 47, 49, 52
see also dichotomy
coherence of learning 68
collaboration, inspiration 108,
115, 125
communicating, perceptions
of librarians 44–5
communication
decision-making process
52–3
dichotomy 52–3
community
defining 62–4
digital environment 74–5
diversity 63–6
exploring 64–6
Google generation 74–5
identifying 61–75
meeting needs 100–1
social-democratic approach
66
technical-rationalist
approach 64–6
understanding 61–75
ways of thinking about 66–9

competing demands, services
62–4

compromises, dichotomy 57

conferences, inspiration 177

congruence expectations,
practice/professional
beliefs 48–9

connections, innovation 144–6

constraints/responses,
professionalism 78–80

constructivist/cognitive
approach, learning 72

constructivist perspective,
teaching approach 70

'consultative tutors' 26

continuing professional
development 2

contrived collegiality, school
culture 67

courses, inspiration 176

creativity, inspiration 103–8

cross-curricular activities,
integration 141–2

cultural sensitivity
dichotomy 54
IFLA 54

cultures, schools' 67–9

curriculum, importance 25–6

data sharing, benchmarking
84–5

decision-making process
communication 52–3
dichotomy 52–3

deputy head, perceptions of
librarians 29–30

determination
innovation 156
inspiration 106–7

development, inspiration
111–12

development planning,
prioritizing 173

dichotomy
ACAS 56–7
awareness 54, 55
beliefs re-examination 57–8
CIPD 57
circumstances 49–54
cognitive dissonance 47, 49,
52
communication 52–3
compromises 57
congruence expectations
48–9
cultural sensitivity 54
decision-making process
52–3

dichotomy (*continued*)
  external pressures 50
  'goalposts' moving 49–51
  intellectual access 54
  Middle East appointment
    50
  misconceptions 49
  mismatches 55–6
  opportunities/threats 51
  origins 53-4
  practice/professional beliefs
    47–59
  prioritizing 57–8
  resolving 55–9
  role-switching 49
  science-strong librarian 48
  threats/opportunities 51
digital environment,
    community 74–5
discourses
  managerialism 4–9
  professionalism 4–15
  social-democracy 11–15
  technical-rationalism 9–11
diversity
  community 63–6
  services 64–6

education levels 166

effectiveness measurement,
    managerialism discourse
    7–9
engagement, integration
    133
English as an additional
    language, service
    considerations 65
enquiry-based learning,
    integration 133
equality emphasis
  services 62
  social-democracy discourse
    12–15
ethical dilemmas, social-
    democracy discourse
    14–15
evidence, innovation 149–51
evidence, using,
    professionalism 83
evolving libraries 33
exhibitions, inspiration 178
external pressures, dichotomy
    50

feedback, meeting needs
    100–1
force field analysis, innovation
    148

fragmented individualism,
    school culture 67
gifted/talented students,
    service considerations 65
'goalposts' moving, dichotomy
    49–51
Google generation,
    community 74–5
government, perceptions of
    librarians 34
governors
    perceptions of librarians
      31–2
    SEF 31
group development,
    professional identity 22–3

'Habits of Mind', integration
    132
Hargreaves, A. 67–8
Headmasters' and
    Headmistresses'
    Conference (HMC),
    innovation 151
headteachers
    deputy head 29–30
    perceptions of librarians
      29–30, 39–40
    work environment 21

HMC *see* Headmasters' and
    Headmistresses'
    Conference
Homework Club,
    professionalism 87
humanistic approach, learning
    72

ideas, inspiration 105–6, 124
IFLA *see* International
    Federation of Library
    Associations
implementation, managing
    change 182
implementation phases,
    managing change
    182–4
inclusion, integration 133
incorporation, managing
    change 183–4
information access,
    social–democracy
    discourse 11–12
information dissemination,
    professionalism 87–8
information literacy
    awareness-raising 37
    integration 129
    professional identity 22

information skills
    integration 131–2
    priority 40
    teaching 37–8, 40
information specialists 26
initiation, managing change
    181–2
initiatives, relationships 96–7
innovation 143-56
    action 146–9
    awards 150–1
    change, managing 151–6
    connections 144–6
    criteria 150–1
    determination 156
    evidence 149–51
    force field analysis 148
    HMC 151
    inspiration 145–6
    leadership 147–9
    managing change 151–6
    planning tools 147–9
    reflective questions 147
    risk-taking 143–4
    scope 151–2
    SWOT analysis 147–8
    VLE 149
innovative solutions,
    professionalism 78–83

inspection process
    ignorance 51–2
    SEF 38
    stock losses 51–2
    teachers 38–9
inspiration 103–26
    assessment for learning
      117–18
    assumptions, questioning
      116–17
    authors' examples 119–21
    awards 109–10
    books 178–9
    change 105, 107
    collaboration 108, 115, 125
    conferences 177
    courses 176
    creativity 103–8
    determination 106–7
    development 111–12
    exhibitions 178
    fitting in 103–7
    ideas 105–6, 124
    innovation 145–6
    from inside ourselves
      113–14
    from inside the school
      114–15
    inspiring others 122–6

inspiration (*continued*)
  journals 178–9
  keeping inspired 111–13
  leadership 122
  levels 107–10
  motivation 112–13, 114–15
  Mozart Effect 106
  music 106
  National Literacy Trust
    108–9
  newspapers 178–9
  online communities 177–8
  open mind 119
  operational level 109–10
  from outside the school
    115–19
  passion 103–6, 114
  persistence 106–7
  plagiarism 111
  possibilities 176–9
  professional groups 176
  Reading Connects project
    108–9
  reality check 121–2
  reflection 113
  responding to professional
    environment 103–7
  searching for 126
  self-help groups 177

  soul food 104
  strategic level 110
  visions 114
  Web 2.0; 123
  websites 178–9
integration 127–42
  achieving 128–31
  Booked Up scheme 141
  cross-curricular activities
    41–2
  engagement 133
  enquiry-based learning 133
  focus 142
  'Habits of Mind' 132
  inclusion 133
  information literacy 129
  information skills, beyond
    131–2
  learning 133
  liaison 139–41
  management team 135–8
  meanings of 127–8
  mediation process 134–5
  mindset 129
  participation 133
  pathways 139–42
  pedagogic relationships
    130–1
  PLTS 129

integration (*continued*)
  schools 72–3, 105
  Science in the News 133
  social aspect 139
  social bookmarking 142
  starting points 132–4
  structure of the school
    135–9
  sustaining 134–5
  teaching team 128–31
  VLE 142
intellectual access
  dichotomy 54
  IFLA 54
International Federation of
  Library Associations
  (IFLA)
  cultural sensitivity 54
  intellectual access 54
  UNESCO/IFLA School
    Libraries' Manifesto
    62
interview data, meeting needs
  100-1

job descriptions
  managerialism discourse
    19–20
  professionalism 18–20

social-democracy discourse
  20
technical-rationalism
  discourse 18-19
journals, inspiration 178–9

keen readers, service
  considerations 65
key change agents, managing
  change 154–6

leadership
  innovation 147–9
  inspiration 122
  services 101–2
learning approaches 69–75
learning, integration 133
leisure users, service
  considerations 65
levels of education 166
liaison, integration 139–41
librarians, perceptions of *see*
  perceptions of librarians
librarians' roles 41–4, 55–6
libraries, evolving 33
library development
  line-management systems
    94
  professionalism 94

library professionals,
  perceptions of librarians
  35–6
line-management systems
  academic status 93
  library development 94
  professionalism 92–5
line managers *see also* support
  staff
  perceptions of librarians
  28–30
  professionalism 92–5
  relationships 93–4
*Literacy across the curriculum and
  Numeracy across the
  curriculum*,
  professionalism 91

manageability, professionalism
  90-1
management team, integration
  135–8
managerialism discourse
  effectiveness measurement
  7–9
  job descriptions 19–20
  personal learning 8–9
  professionalism 4–9, 19–20
  tensions 5–6

managing change 151–6
  implementation 182
  implementation phases
  182–4
  implementing change
  152
  incorporation 183–4
  initiation 181–2
  innovation 151–6
  key change agents 154–6
  nature of your organization
  152
  People's Network Change
  Management Toolkit 153
  principles 153, 181–5
  prioritizing activities 152–3
  process 153, 181–5
  Toolkit 153
  tools 180
  whole school processes
  147–9, 154–6
  working with people 153
Maslow's hierarchy of
  needs, motivation 73–4
mediation process, integration
  134–5
meeting needs
  community 100–1
  feedback 100–1

merging of library and IT
  centre 51
Middle East appointment,
  dichotomy 50
mindset, integration 129
misconceptions, dichotomy
  49
mismatches
  dichotomy 55–6
  roles 55–6
motivation
  inspiration 112–13, 114–15
  Maslow's hierarchy of
    needs 73–4
Mozart Effect, inspiration 106
music, inspiration 106

National Literacy Trust
  inspiration 178–9

older students
  service considerations 65
online communities
  inspiration 177–8
open mind
  inspiration 119
operational level
  inspiration 109–10
opportunities/threats

dichotomy 51
organizations' strategic views
  67

parents
  perceptions of librarians
    32–3
  roles 32–3
  service considerations 65
participation
  integration 133
passion
  inspiration 103–6, 114
pedagogic relationships
  integration 130–1
*Pedagogy and Practice: teaching
  and learning in secondary
  schools* 36
peer involvement
  professionalism 81
peer reviews
  benchmarking 84–5
People's Network Change
  Management Toolkit
  managing change 153
perceptions of librarians 25–46
  communicating 44–5
  deputy head 29–30
  government 34

perceptions of librarians
    (*continued*)
  governors 31–2
  headteachers 29–30, 39–40
  implications 44–5
  influences 36–40
  library professionals 35–6
  line managers 28–30
  parents 32–3
  public 34–5
  publicizing 44–5
  students 30–1
  teachers 27–8, 36–9, 41–4,
    170
persistence
  inspiration 106–7
personal learning
  managerialism discourse 8–9
Personal, Learning and
    Thinking Skills (PLTS)
  integration 129
personal vision
  professionalism 99
plagiarism
  inspiration 111
planning
  development planning 173
  professionalism 89–90
planning tools

innovation 147–9
PLTS *see* Personal, Learning
    and Thinking Skills
policy documents
  *Literacy across the curriculum
  and Numeracy across the
  curriculum* 91
poor use of library 33
positioning
  professionalism 77–8
positivity
  professionalism 80–3
possibilities
  professionalism 78–80
post-modernist interpretations
  professionalism 15–17
practice/professional beliefs
  dichotomy 47–59
principles
  managing change 153, 181–5
prioritizing
  development planning 173
  dichotomy 57–8
  professionalism 89–92, 97
  relationships 97
  school priorities 89–92
  student priorities 98–9
  teaching approaches 71
  user priorities 89–92

prioritizing activities
  managing change 152–3
process
  managing change 153,
    181–5
professional beliefs/practice
  dichotomy 47–59
professional groups
  inspiration 176
professional identity 22–4
  cognitive authority 23
  group development 22–3
  information literacy 22
professionalism 1–24, 77–102
    see also services
  academic status 93
  audit trail 81
  balance 92
  benchmarking 83–6
  CILIP 2
  clerical support 82–3
  constraints/responses 78–80
  discourses 4–15
  evidence, using 83
  Homework Club 87
  influences 18–21
  information dissemination
    87–8
  innovative solutions 78–83

job descriptions 18–20
library development 94
line–management systems
    92–5
line managers 92–5
*Literacy across the curriculum
  and Numeracy across the
  curriculum* 91
manageability 90–1
managerialism discourse
    4–9, 19–20
meanings of 2–4
peer involvement 81
personal vision 99
planning 89–90
positioning 77–8
positivity 80–3
possibilities 78–80
post-modernist
    interpretations 15–17
prioritizing 89–92, 97
professional identity 22–4
relationships 93–7
responses/constraints 78–80
roles 88–9
school priorities 89–92
social-democracy discourse
    11–15, 20
students, learning from 97–9

professionalism (*continued*)
  successful school librarians
    24
  support staff 82–3
  SWOT analysis 79–80
  technical-rationalism
    discourse 9–11, 18–19
  threats 3
  user priorities 89–92
  views 17–24
  visions 16–17, 99
  work environment 21
  workforce remodelling
    95
  working with others 86–8
public
  perceptions of librarians
    34–5
publicizing
  perceptions of librarians
    44–5

questionnaire data
  meeting needs 100–1

Reading Connects project
  inspiration 108–9
reality check
  inspiration 121–2

reductionism
  technical-rationalism
    discourse 10–11
reflection
  inspiration 113
reflective questions
  innovation 147
relationships
  developing 77
  initiatives 96–7
  line managers 93–4
  prioritizing 97
  professionalism 93–7
  timing 96
reluctant readers
  service considerations 65
responses/constraints
  professionalism 78–80
risk-taking
  innovation 143–4
role-switching
  dichotomy 49
roles *see also* perceptions of
    librarians
  librarians' 41–4, 55–6
  mismatches 55–6
  professionalism 88–9
  stock losses 51–2

school priorities
  professionalism 89–92
schools' cultures 67–9
Science in the News
  integration 133
science-strong librarian
  dichotomy 48
SEF *see* self evaluation form
self-evaluation example 174–5
self evaluation form (SEF)
  governors 31
  inspection process 38
self-evaluation questions
  school library 168–9
self-help groups
  inspiration 177
services *see also* professionalism
  competing demands 62–4
  diversity 64–6
  equality emphasis 62
  leadership 101–2
  user considerations 65
skills, information *see*
    information skills
social aspect
  integration 139
social bookmarking
  integration 142
social-democracy discourse

equality emphasis 12–15
ethical dilemmas 14–15
information access 11–12
job descriptions 20
professionalism 11–15, 20
social-democratic approach
  community 66
soul food
  inspiration 104
special educational needs
  service considerations 65
staff, support *see* support staff
standards
  benchmarking 85–6
statistics
  meeting needs 100–1
stock
  changing 33
stock losses
  inspection process 51–2
  roles 51–2
strategic level
  inspiration 110
strategic views
  organizations' 67
students
  learning from 97–9
  perceptions of librarians
    30–1

students (*continued*)
  priorities 98–9
successful school librarians
  professionalism 24
support staff *see also* line
    managers
  professionalism 82–3
  service considerations 65
SWOT analysis
  example 171–2
  innovation 147–8
  professionalism 79–80

tasks defining
  technical-rationalism
    discourse 9–10
teachers
  inspection process 38–9
  perceptions of librarians
    27–8, 36–9, 41–4, 170
teaching approaches 69–75
  behaviourist approach
    69–70
  constructivist perspective 70
  prioritizing 71
teaching staff
  service considerations 65
teaching team
  integration 128–31

technical-rationalism
  discourse
    criticisms 10–11
    job descriptions 18–19
    professionalism 9–11, 18–19
    reductionism 10–11
    tasks defining 9–10
technical-rationalist approach
  community 64–6
threats/opportunities
  dichotomy 51
timing
  relationships 96
tools
  managing change 153, 180
  planning tools, innovation
    147–9

UNESCO/IFLA School
  Libraries' Manifesto 62
  benchmarking 85–6
user priorities
  professionalism 89–92

views
  professionalism 17–24
virtual learning environment
  (VLE)
  innovation 149

virtual learning environment
(*continued*)
integration 142
visions
inspiration 114
personal vision 99
professionalism 16–17, 99
VLE *see* virtual learning
environment

Web 2.0
inspiration 123
websites 166
inspiration 178–9
Wenger, E. 68

whole school processes
managing change 147–9,
154–6
work environment
headteachers 21
professionalism 21
workforce remodelling
professionalism 95
working with others
professionalism 86–8
working with people
managing change 153

younger students
service considerations 65

Libraries Designed for Kids
Nolan Lushington

How do you set about planning and designing a library for children or teenagers? How should it be different from a library intended for adults, and how can you get the right kind of help from designers and architects?

Get the 'inside story' from an experienced library design consultant on creating those special spaces in your library that promote and encourage children's and young adults' curiosity, learning, and reading – and support their lifelong love of books and information.

Nolan Lushington covers the complete planning process from concept to 'grand opening', guiding you through the technical aspects of design and construction and the finer points of lighting, acoustics, furnishings, equipment, multimedia areas, youth areas, and much more. Key topics include:

- improving service by design
- innovative children's library models
- planning a new children's library
- assessing physical needs
- design considerations
- organizing the children's area
- entrances, displays, graphics and lighting
- age-related design
- designing programme, activity and staff areas
- furnishings and equipment
- quick fixes and common mistakes.

The helpful appendices offer case studies and lists of suppliers, architects and further information.

Whether you're a children's or youth librarian, library director, school facilities planner – or indeed an architect or designer – you'll discover valuable, practical tips and insights to help you create that inviting environment called the library.

Nolan Lushington is a library design consultant and President of Lushington Consultants, Hartford CT. He is Chairman of the American Library Association Buildings and Equipment Section and a juror of the ALA Building Awards.

2008; 184pp; paperback; 978-1-85604-657-2; £44.95

Delivering the Best Start
A guide to early years libraries

Carolynn Rankin and Avril Brock

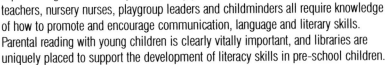

The Early Years Foundation Stage (EYFS) is now statutory in the UK for children from birth to five years, and other countries are experiencing similar developments; early years librarians, teachers, nursery nurses, playgroup leaders and childminders all require knowledge of how to promote and encourage communication, language and literary skills. Parental reading with young children is clearly vitally important, and libraries are uniquely placed to support the development of literacy skills in pre-school children.

This book provides an understanding of how children develop such skills through enjoyable and meaningful learning experiences, and is a pioneering practical guide for library and information professionals involved in planning and delivering services in early years libraries. Drawing on the authors' underpinning contemporary research and examples from current best practice, it will equip practitioners with a broad range of knowledge and ideas. Key areas covered include:

- take them to the library: the role of the early years professional
- people and partnerships: working across disciplinary boundaries, and how to involve parents and carers
- buildings, design and space: the children's libraries of the future
- resources for early years libraries: books, toys and other delights
- reaching your audience: the librarian's role
- planning and organizing: projects and reading sessions.

User-friendly and accessible, each chapter is clearly structured and sets out the key issues for practitioners, scenarios offering insights into these, and practical ideas and resources for service provision. The book also includes case studies of successful pre-school library initiatives in a variety of global settings, useful information about relevant organizations, and links to helpful websites.

This valuable text is essential reading for all library and information professionals working with young children – whether those with responsibility for the strategic planning of services, or those involved in delivering them at community level. Essential for students of library and information studies or childhood studies, and practitioners undertaking NVQ qualifications, it also provides a sound background in early years literacy and provision for a range of local authority practitioners, such as nursery teachers and children's centre managers.

2008; 208pp; paperback; 978-1-85604-610-7; £39.95

Digital Consumers

Reshaping the information professions

David Nicholas and Ian Rowlands, editors

The information professions – librarianship, archives, publishing and, to some extent, journalism – have been rocked by the digital transition that has led to disintermediation, easy access and massive information choice. Information now forms a consumer commodity with many diverse information producers engaged in the market.

There is a need for a new belief system that will help information professionals survive and engage in a ubiquitous information environment, where they are no longer the dominant players, nor, indeed, the suppliers of first choice. The aim of this thought-provoking book is to provide that overarching vision, built on hard evidence rather than on PowerPoint 'puff'. An international, cross-sectoral team of contributors has been assembled for this purpose. Key strategic areas covered include:

- the digital consumer: an introduction and philosophy
- the digital information marketplace and its economics: the end of exclusivity
- the e-shopper: the growth of the informed purchaser
- the library in the digital age
- the psychology of the digital information consumer
- the information-seeking behaviour of the digital consumer: case study – the virtual scholar
- the Google generation: myths and realities about young people's digital information behaviour
- trends in digital information consumption and the future.
- where do we go from here?

No information professional or student can afford not to read this far-reaching and important book.

2008; 240pp; hardback; ISBN 978-1-85604-651-0;£39.95

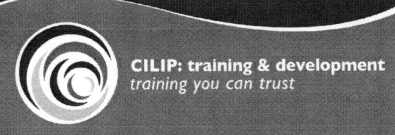